CLOWN CANTOS

BARBARA MOSSBERG

California laureate/City of Pacific Grove
Poet in Residence Emerita

ILLUSTRATIONS by CHRISTINE CROZIER

CLOWN CANTOS
by Barbara Mossberg
Illustrations by Christine Crozier

Cover Design: Janet Marcroft
Cover Image: © Barbara Mossberg 2024
Sculpture by Circle City Metalworks Co.
Back cover painting, oil: Barbara Mossberg,
Autobiography: © Barbara Mossberg 2019

First Edition 2025
© Barbara Mossberg 2024
ALL RIGHTS RESERVED

PRINT: ISBN 978-1-953120-83-0
EBOOK: ISBN 978-1-053120-84-7
Published by Park Place Publications
Pacific Grove, California

ALSO BY BARBARA MOSSBERG

Emily Dickinson: When A Writer Is a Daughter (Indiana, 1982)
If You Promise to Let Me Write This Down I Promise You an Ice Cream
    (Buddy Press, 1988)
The Physics of Purple (Buddy Press, 1997)
Sometimes the Woman in the Mirror Is Not You, and other hopeful news postings
    (Finishing Line Press, 2015)
*Here for the Present: A Grammar of Happiness in the Present Imperfect, Live
    from the Poet's Perch* (Park Place Publications, 2021)

Mossberg's poems and essays also appear in: *Frontier Poetry, Tupelo
    Quarterly, New Millenium Writings, Cider House Press, Cedar Street
    Times, The Emily Dickinson Bulletin, The Dickinson Journal, What
    Would Henry Do?, John Muir and Friends, Huffington Post Arts&Culture,
    The Presidency, The Chronicle of Higher Education, The National
    Teaching and Learning Forum, Educational Record, Proceedings for 5th
    International Conference on Women in Higher Education, Women's Studies,
    Calapooya 8, The Fulbright Difference, Proceedings from the Conference
    on the 2nd Nuclear Age and the Academy, Roots and Renewals: Writings
    by Bicentennial Fulbright Professors, Historical Studies and Literary
    Criticism*, and others.

CLOWN CANTOS

Meditations on Fellow Being
and Mortal Happiness
Pondering This Our Life

*Everything is Alive
in its Own Way,
Singing*

To Christer, an Everything,
champion of the untamed,
among the birds and the bees and the thunder
and the lions and beaver
and wolverine and pickerel and muskrat,
all there is to love and not know and only feel
wonder and humble gratitude —
i.e., a Fellow Mortal,
who must be sung

and

Nicolino aka Nico Moss
who brought me to *Radiotopia's*
Ian Chillag's "Everything Is Alive".
Whom I wrote a song about on the day he was born,
Saying, You're our very own family Clown,
and is alive
in his own way,
singing

and

Sophia/SophySophie
actual singer on stages since the age of six,
who will kindly join me in any tune, or dance;
poet, artist, illustrator, photographer,
DOJ Child Advocacy AAG for State of Oregon
and
everyone who knows her would say
she speaks Cantos and animates this book.

CLOWN CANTOS

Pondering My Fellow Mortals

*Everything Is Alive
in Its Own Way,
Singing*

Events must be sung and sing themselves – Ralph Waldo Emerson
Everything Is Alive – Ian Chillag, Radiotopia
Everything Is Beautiful in Its Own Way – Dolly Parton

A little Madness in the Spring
Is wholesome even for the King,
But God be with the Clown –
Who ponders this tremendous scene –
This whole Experiment of Green –
As if it were his own!
– Emily Dickinson

CANTOS

Singers, the Sung, and the Pondered

9	**Author's Note**	
15	**Foreword**	

A LITTLE MADNESS IN THE SPRING

30	**Rock**	Fool's Gold
36	**Spider**	In Which I Happily Give Up
40	**Camel**	*Camel Escapes and "Stomps" Man in Southern California* (The Associated Press, Saturday, February 15, 2014)
44	**Rooster**	To All We Secretly Love

48	**Blueberry**	I Forgive Gravity
52	**Lake**	Washing the Lake
58	**Cow**	*This is the Day the Lord Has Made: Do You Pass Up Heaven on Earth?*
62	**Bear**	Night Hunger, Wild Hunger
68	**Great Blue Heron**	Quantum Happiness at Charlie's Boat House

Is Wholesome Even for the King

76	**Crane**	When I Think of You I Remember the Cranes in the Helsinki Zoo
80	**Lion**	In That Same Time
84	**Log**	Terra Incognita
86	**Squirrel / Fox**	Resurrection Shenanigans
92	**Pigeon / Oysters**	The pigeon collecting commemorative poppies in a field where soldiers died. To build a nest.
96	**Coho**	When Edible Is a Happy Ending for All

But God Be With the Clown

100	**Mouse**	The Ridiculous Relentless Cheerfulness of a Mouse
104	**Dragonfly**	How I'm Taught Green
106	**Glacier**	Dining on Glacier

110	**Deer**	You Have Seen This Scene in Sixty Paintings Except the Tangerine and the Deer
114	**Koi**	The Koi Loves Me Back
116	**Eggplant**	Milanese Turns Out to Be Gateway Grief
120	**Cat**	Animals That Saw You

Who Ponders This Tremendous Scene

124	**Bee**	"Does This Pollen Make My Butt Look Big?"
126	**Turkey**	I mean God! To have a turkey in your day
132	**Turnip**	There Comes a Time for Happiness
136	**Goldfish**	The Improbability of Orange
140	**Loon**	Why
142	**River**	When I Die You Don't Have to Divert the River for Me
146	**Whale**	This Thing We Call Friendship is Bigger Than We Know
150	**Octopus**	How I Became a Vegetarian
154	**River**	You Are Not Not Moving in a Happening Illimitably World

This Whole Experiment of Green

158	**Pigeon**	The Existentialist Casserole: A Natural History

170	**Buffalo**	Buffalo Poem
172	**Bear (again)**	A bear attacks a woman. She fights it off with her laptop.
176	**Worm**	You Have This Chance
180	**Flamingo**	My Not My Flamingo
184	**Earth/Me**	In Which It Is Revealed I Am Earth
188	**Sunshine**	$E=mc^2$: For example

As if it were his own!—Emily Dickinson

190	**Nebulae**	Frolic King Among the Nebulae
194	**River**	Don't Even Read This
198	**Jacaranda**	I Am Telling You This
202	**Basket**	Natural History Does Not Include My Plans to Fly
206	**Petal**	*The song sings itself* (Wm. Carlos Williams)
208	**Hummingbird**	On Being Human
212	**Turtle, et. al.**	*Alive Again Today*

217	**A Note from the Illustrator**
218	**A Note from My Mother**
219	**A Note from My Son**
220	**Acknowledgements**
225	**Human** Fat Lady Flying
227	**Author Information**

Author's Note

I saw a worm. I won't say it changed my life. Rather, it made clear my life, or, roiled, my thinking about what it is about my life and all our lives that is worth saving. Worth fighting for. Rooting for. Shaken, lit, moved at the mystery of being connected to such a phenomenal being, I proceeded to my office, and in the normally hectic hour before class, I wrote. I had to tell you. Yesterday, driving, I saw a turkey on the sidewalk. I pulled over. I pondered, like Emily Dickinson's Clown. I was talking turkey; I was all over myself in amazement at what Dante calls *this our life*. I was beside myself, undone by happiness.

And I had to tell you.

I had to tell you. Isn't this the plot of so many of our stories—this urge, this excitement, this struggle? Gilgamesh, in 2700 BCE atop a wall. Homer, imploring the Muse to sing to him/her/them to help tell the story of Odysseus, the story that must be told. Dante, having to tell us what happened that day he found himself lost on his path, even though just remembering it practically kills him. Emily Dickinson, wanting to tell us *how the sun rose*, and having *so much to tell* Dear March when she finally comes, and tell us Nature's News, the "Bulletins all day" and other immortal news: "I tell it you." Henry David Thoreau's essential accounting of his life for our sakes. Mark Twain's Huck, overcoming odds to tell us in his own words. Sojourner Truth. Maya Angelou, how the caged bird sings. Ralph Ellison's black-and-blues in *Invisible Man*.

William Carlos Williams, his heart aroused:

There is something
                        something urgent
I have to say to you
            and you alone . . .

And so
         with fear in my heart
                  I drag it out
and keep on talking
            for I dare not stop.

                                    Listen while I talk on
against time. . . .

Only give me time,
        time to recall them
                before I shall speak out.
Give me time,
        time. . . .
Hear me out.
Do not turn away.
I have learned much in my life
        from books
                and out of them
about love. . . .
        I come, my sweet,
                to sing to you!
My heart rouses
        thinking to bring you news
                of something
that concerns you
        and concerns many men. Look at
                what passes for the new.
You will not find it there but in
        despised poems.
                It is difficult
to get the news from poems
        yet men die miserably every day
                for lack
of what is found there.
        Hear me out
                for I too am concerned
and every man
        who wants to die at peace in his bed
                besides.

Hear me out. Listen. Give me time. Something urgent I have to say to you.

What is in these poems that we die without? Williams' claims of life and death stakes in tales to be told may be explained because he is a physician, with life and death on his mind and blood in his hands every day. Rx poems, to heal us, to save us: I think of Samuel Taylor Coleridge's *Rime of the Ancient Mariner*, and the tragic fate of his poor old narrator who has to tell us, warning us to take to heart his own doomed story of his deadly encounter with an albatross.

What would make me stop what I'm doing in the middle of my life when I see a worm, or practically end my life pulling over in busy traffic thrilled at the sight of a turkey, overcome with having to tell you? Perhaps it is the poet's curse—or blessing, but this sense of excitement and significance about our world that makes me stop what I'm doing to reflect with you is as old as the hills, or at least, as the humans living on them. It may make for a trying companion, remote right next to you, lost in a fog, then interrupting your Real Life with a writer's urgent news. It may make me a clown. But it's a thing—as we say. Certainly my life is changed from a sense of consequential news. It is Wordsworth's lyrics about the rainbow that teach me how to see—with wonder and awe; how to experience—exuberantly: *my heart leaps up when I behold*. In the breeze I see trees as spirits *leaping greenly* because of e.e. cummings' sonnet, "i thank You God for most this amazing."

Richard Eberhart's groundhog, Mark Doty's green-shelled crab, D.H. Lawrence's whale, Henry David Thoreau's muskrat. Elizabeth Bishop's fish—ah, *rainbow*: our literature is a taxonomy of astonishment for whom Robert Burns calls our *Fellow Mortals*. I think of Emily Dickinson's pondering Clown, beholding earth as a "tremendous scene." We are taught ecstasy in a vision that connects us to earthly being. In each other's writing, perhaps, is a magic mirror into which we peer for possibilities of seeing our own shimmering lives.

In transformational visions, on the air, on stage, and on the page, we are challenged to see ourselves connected to . . . everything. If I stop for a worm, surely it is because of Robert Burns' "To a Mouse," written just after the American and French revolutions, and just as revolutionary in expanding our sense of enfranchisement, of civic equality and belonging: a so-called pest is recognized as an *earth-born companion*. We are challenged to view a lowly mouse empathically as a Fellow Mortal. Emily Dickinson expands this sense of Fellow Mortal to earth itself. Written when America is being systematically deforested, Emily Dickinson's noble Clown shows us how to view our trodden, downtrodden, earth as inextricably connected to us: he "ponders . . . as if it were his own!" It is a sanctified wisdom: "God be with the Clown!"

In our own day, Radiotopia's program of Ian Chillag's *Everything Is Alive* is a companion profound philosophy, asking modern-day Shakespearian clowns to consider the "life" of all objects—soap, lampposts, off-brand cola, with empathy and compassion. Our empathy is expanding exponentially, like the universe itself. NPR host Chillag, in "Wait Wait Don't Tell Me," celebrates the news of us quirky weird humans. But his *EIA* brings news of the inanimate—so called—-beings' take on existence and humans. It is an existential romp.

Added to the idea of everything—*everything*—being alive, that we share existence and therefore mortality with all entities, in the faith of e.e. cummings' sonnet "i thank You God for most this amazing," *everything* is alive beyond fellow mortal life: "i who have died am alive again today." We are connected through resurrection, immortal resilience. This kind of hope is based on Henry David Thoreau's "infinite expectation of the dawn" in *Walden*, which ends with his own connection with nature that lets him know his own day is like the sun, in which there is "more day to dawn." He has "more lives to live," and e.e. cummings takes this further with him being "alive again today."

Then our own Dolly Parton says that "Everything Is Beautiful in Its Own Way," a perspective on our lives that is not only wholly expansive and inclusive but celebratory. We all are alive, holy, and beautiful Fellow Mortals, fellow immortals.

Stopping for a worm: this collection of memoir sketches of earthly encounters is my homage to the writers' lens. I take heart in science and poetry of the oneness of all wildly individual lives, sharing a fate of everything "alive in its own way," "alive again today."

Yes, worms. And we stop together for all Fellow being, no-footed, one-footed, two-footed, four-footed, gilled, winged, fanged, orbiting, pulsing, erupting, melting, inanimate, looked over, and considered "over"—not so fast!

In this circus of being, "us" is beyond life and death. Epic poet Walt Whitman extends his *Song of Myself* to every kind of being, all operating according to the same laws. Albert Einstein agrees with his own poem, $e=mc2$. Dante's epic Cantos refer to *this our life*—not *his* life, *our* life.

Thus Chillag extends Dante's vision of human belonging beyond mortal being, of empathy out into the material quantum, and Parton gathers the lot of us under the quantum umbrella of beauty—something mysterious and wonderful to revere, to behold, to respect. Emily Dickinson's Clown ponders "this tremendous scene … as if it were his own!" To see a Fellow Mortal is to look into the mirror of our being. We are so alive, again and again. And lovely. And loving. And beloved. And often so sad, and sorry.

Stopping to ponder such poignant and hopeful visions of infinite being: what I have to tell you is my own Clown happiness.

The theater world has a saying when things have become chaos on stage: "send in the clowns." We need the Clown in our crises, not so much diverting us with arts, but perhaps pointing to greater truths. In a world that is as dark as light, and fraught and filled with fright, we hear Ralph Waldo Emerson console and inspire us with the idea that no matter what there is "alway, alway music." It's almost as if we can find it. But the role of the writer in this is at the fore, when he says, or commands, "Events must be sung and sing themselves." So I am trying, in this vision of the fellowship of infinite being, to make every Fellow Mortal I encounter as a Clown an *event that must be sung*. The challenge is not only to see everything as alive, as we each experience being, but to imagine how a body sings itself, if we listen. If we ponder. If we say *tell me*.

Here now are characters on my path that tell me, that I sing in Cantos of driveway improv and rest stop flash memoirs of engagements with our world phenomena, when this world just comes upon me, manifests in worms and turkeys and breakaway camels and spiders, in wondrous ways like stars to wise men, or angels to the six-year-old William Blake, or worrisome, as Dante found himself facing wild beasts, or glorious, as John Muir experiences the wild world: *The Glory! The Glory!* he pants, on top of some peak I would be afraid to climb (but not you).

But sometimes we must climb, out of darkness, out of the woods. As Dante and Virgil climb the peak and reach the morning sunlight, Paradise, we go together, my beloved writers and you, and we sing each other as Fellow Mortals, *You Are My Sunshine*.

Clown Cantos: Everything is alive in its own way, singing.

In this circus of memoir with a Clown narrator and Ringmasters Dante, Dolly Parton, Ian Chillag, Einstein, Emily Dickinson, Emerson and the Transcendentalists, e.e. cummings, a whole and holy host of philosophical performers, a starry troupe, and you, Reader—an *event that must be sung*.

I have to tell you.

        I believe in those wing'd purposes,
And acknowledge red, yellow, white, playing within me,
And consider green and violet and the tufted crown intentional,
And do not call the tortoise unworthy because she is not something else,

And the jay in the woods never studied the gamut,
        yet trills pretty well to me,
And the look of the bay mare shames silliness out of me . . .
The sharp-hoof'd moose of the north, the cat on the house-sill,
        the chickadee, the prairie-dog,
The litter of the grunting sow as they tug at her teats,
The brood of the turkey-hen and she with her half-spread wings,
I see in them and myself the same old law.
        WALT WHITMAN, *Leaves of Grass*

Let me go where'er I will
I hear a sky-born music still:
It sounds from all things old,
It sounds from all things young,
From all that's fair, from all that's foul,
Peals out a cheerful song.

It is not only in the rose,
It is not only in the bird,
Not only where the rainbow glows.
Nor in the song of woman heard,
But in the darkest meanest things . . .
There alway, alway something sings . . .

But in the mud and scum of things
There alway, alway something sings.
        RALPH WALDO EMERSON, "Music"

Foreword

In telling of one's life, in its late middle, when many mysterious and serious and hilarious things have been encountered, and many things lost, and many things found, and hopefully a few things still to come, Dante's *The Divine Comedy* is a good place to start.

> *Nel mezzo del cammin di nostra vita*
> In the middle of the journey of this our life

So begins Canto One: *in the middle of the journey*, singing of *this our life*. Dante doesn't say, *my* life. He says, *our* life. I'm interested in what a man rhyming in Italian in the 1300s—before Advil and coffee and AZO—recognizes as *our* story, yours and mine, as if our stories are the same, and telling his, lighting ours.

The story he feels is all of ours is daunting and dire. *Inferno*—actual hell; *Purgatory*—death *and* still suffering; *Paradise*—the light at last, it cannot come soon enough. Most of his *this our life* story deals with darkness. His first lines are plight and fright. He's in the dark woods, he can't make out his path, and what's more, he's facing fanged and snarling beasts.

It doesn't sound especially comic. I'm in, though, because the title *Comedy* promises a happy ending, and I have a very low bar when it comes to happiness. I'll take it even though it comes late to the scene.

It's when he says, *Ah me!*—

> Ah me! how hard a thing it is to say
> What was this forest savage, rough, and stern,
> Which the very thought of renews the fear.
>
> So bitter is it, death is little more;
> But of the good to treat, which there I found,
> Speak will I of the other things I saw there.

—that sigh, that gets me: the earnest effort to tell us his story, all of it; even though it ended well, it practically kills him to think back on it. How to tell it? Why engage this struggle? Dante brings us backstage—back *page*, to confide in his storyteller's challenge. He goes straight to miracle.

At his greatest moment of crisis wondering *what will become of me*, out of the shadows appears a rescue-engine to lead him to the light—a writer! (Of course.) A fellow writer! Someone whose own writing shaped him, someone he loves to read, someone who sings to him. Virgil, the epic poet of *The Aeneid,* written in Latin a thousand years earlier, is immediate to Dante, as perhaps Rumi, or Emily Dickinson, and Thoreau, and Whitman, Cervantes, Rostand, and so many others—and Dante himself, are to me. You'll see. So many writers inside me, at my bedside, in my backpack, who are how I think, who travel with me in the MRI, the hospital nursery, the crematorium, the classroom, the waiting room, the plane, the green room, the page.

Poke me, and out from under my guise as a foibled old lady flies a flock of ready Virgils—perhaps the plural of Virgil would be *epic*. An *epic of Virgils*, to save me.

I am thinking of Einstein, a musician and poet, who wrote $e=mc2$, that wild notion that everything is connected. Dolly Parton singing harmony to Einstein in *everything is beautiful in its own way*. Ian Chillag on *Radiotopia* proclaiming *Everything Is Alive*—and he means, everything.

We are in the dark woods, yes, and things look bad. But help is at hand. There is *an epic of Virgils* deputized to lead us to the light. We have a contingent—a regiment—a roster: it could be Mary Oliver, or Joy Harjo, or Audre Loude, or Amanda Gorman, or Awkward-Cameron Rich, or Bayo Akomolafe, or Mark Doty, fractals of a holy book.

It's all equation elation

I do the $e=mc2$. According to the Special Theory of Relativity, the impossibility/possibility that *this* is *that*. I hear miraculous engineering of connecting in Radiotopia's *Everything Is Alive,* where Ian and a chosen conversant, perhaps a can of off brand cola, or bar of soap, or lamppost, or Halloween pumpkin, explore the experience of living as poignantly or even more poignantly, as any human with a great heart and reflective mind. People weep at the tale of Louis the Can of Cola. And Dolly Parton's *Everything is beautiful,* is singing the same thing, that everything is connected and alive and *beautiful in its own way*, on its own terms, in its own skin, equal, in a vibrational way of being.

Yes, it's $e=mc2$, physics, quantum theory, but also, this is poetry's realm and lifeblood, the metaphor! It is the metaphor that accomplishes miracles of connection, the mind's ability to see things wholly, to put things together.

And indeed, long before Einstein's famous revelation of belonging, Robert Burns has a revolutionary vision: he sees a *Fellow Mortal* in a pest, a mouse whom he calls his *earth-born companion*.

Half a century and a continent away, Walt Whitman sees feathered and shelled lives and his own life operating according to *the same old law*.

Millennia before that, the Mayans said, *You are my other me*. And today in Latin American culture, *mi casa es su casa*. My house is your house.

Then there is Emily Dickinson's news of Spring, and a Clown who sees it, not as dark and fearsome, not as a gateway to hell. Rather, it is a "Divine Comedy."

> A little madness in the Spring
> Is wholesome even for the King,
> But God be with the Clown—
> Who ponders this tremendous scene—
> This whole Experiment of Green—
> As if it were his own!

In the poem I think of as her anthem throwing down the green eco gauntlet, it's our earth the Clown fancies he owns. He sees *this scene* of ours as *tremendous*, what Dickinson calls an *Experiment of Green*. Dickinson's sciency spiritual world is not a finished thing: it's still happening, becoming, emergent. It's not done, it's not over. It is world without end, limitless, infinite, green as green can be, growing, alive, and alive, and alive again.

In such a viewpoint, the world for all its pain and terror is *tremendous*. Dickinson's God approves of this never ending way of seeing this our life. *God be with the Clown*.

We tend to dismiss a Clown as not serious, but this Clown *ponders* earth *[A] s if it were his own!* In her body of more than two thousand poems, Dickinson hardly ever uses an exclamation point. But this power punctuation shows how important is the Clown's way of seeing.

The Philosopher Clown?

So for me, rapt in the spiritual pyrotechnics of Einstein, Ian Chillag, and Dolly Parton, our world's angels are singing with Dante, and Robert Burns, Thoreau, Walt Whitman, Emily Dickinson, Emerson, and so many others.

In each of these poet's lines, we are being given guides like Dante's Virgil, guidelines for how to see the light of our world. *Alive. Alive again today! Tremendous! Whole! Beautiful in its own way! Everything!* A slew of epic rescues when we feel submerged in struggle.

When we put together these ideas from all over the world and across time, that one person's story is all our story, that we are all the same being, and beautiful at that, no matter how fraught and full of muck or feathers, Emerson's saying it all *must be sung*, that's . . . a bit much on a busy day, I get that, scientists' quirk and artists' kook, but also, isn't it amazing? If we see things *as our own*—as if they are us, as if we are each other, literally, wouldn't that matter in how we experience ourselves alive, and how we treat each other? Seeing each other as *kin*, wouldn't we be *kind*? Wouldn't we want to save everyone we could, since each other's lives is our own fate?

And if Ian Chillag in his ingenious *Radiotopia* program is right, that "Everything Is Alive," it isn't just us with two legs, or us with four legs as earthborn companions, or us with wings and gills operating to the same laws, it's rocks and galaxies and glaciers and rivers and dust. It's pencils and coffee. And the mug.

Perhaps because I have spent most of my life being somewhat like the Clown reveling in *this tremendous scene*, I feel lifted by these songs and formulas and poems and pronouncements and autobiographical confessions of this book's epigraphs. If everything is the same thing, we are each other and each other's. This cozy quantum interdependence gives me great hope in our mutual fates to end up as sunbeams, and in the meantime to see light in our world, no matter how dark, to hear something always *alway singing*, as Emerson says in *Music*, no matter the muck. To belong to each other. To be each other's sunshine. To see everything alive, everything.

A Naked Virgil Apparition

If everything is alive, then nothing is not alive.

This must have been what I was realizing. I was naked, in a trance, entranced, in a sauna in northern Finland, when John Muir, who up to that point I did not know, personally, now appeared, also naked:

> He thinks he is clinging to a rock, he thinks it is alive, he lets go and is flying, trees dance and rocks breathe, space is alive as any river, he thinks he is a pink rock warmed by sun, he has lost track of who is alive and what moves and what isn't alive and what doesn't move what has bark and what has limbs and what has heart, but he knows that nothing is always there. So that must mean everything moves, something must move it, he thinks of what or who moves us. He is so little, but he is so ecstatic, his vision of glory is huge as El Capitan.
> —*Book Me, Sir: John Muir Takes a Sauna with the Naked Ladies of Kuopio,* Barbara Mossberg

The heated vision of everything being alive in its own way and the joy that comes from this recognition became the basis for this book.

John Muir was my surprise Virgil in the steaming smoky sauna in the woods, and two sentences into his heated hymns makes you look around for angels, you are so sure you are in Paradise. But how was it he came to me so unbidden? I grew up in the campfire programs of Yosemite National Park, which he imagined and fought to help create. My high school had his name. But John Muir wasn't taught and to my knowledge I had not read him, and yet, here I am, clearly baptized in his vision.

The writer who I was really thinking of in northern Finland as a Fulbrighter trying to interpret American culture was Henry David Thoreau. To me Thoreau is the ultimate Clown, pondering in his own way, making his woods the epicenter of epiphany of who we are and what we are supposed to be doing with our lives—seeing what is tremendous and beautiful and *us*. He had to go away from all of us at the kitchen table, at the door, in order to find us—and himself. "*I went to the woods to live deliberately . . . and not discover at the end of my life I have not lived at all.*"*(Walden)* John Muir was reading Ralph Waldo Emerson whom I quote here and whose ideas about everything being sung I am trying to answer in my own way, and Robert Burns' "To a Mouse," that breakthrough poem of empathy and companion with Fellow Mortals, pests and all. He sang his fellow Scotsman Bobby Burns. And he was reading Thoreau. He was reading Thoreau so thoroughly that his famous words on wilderness are often inseparable from Thoreau's Clown cantos in letter and spirit.

Send in the Clowns

I reflect that whether it is Einstein or Dolly Parton or Ian Chillag or all the singers of "You Are My Sunshine" (and who is not?), they each inform my sense of the transformational Clown we encounter in Emily Dickinson's vision. The Clown has a quantum vision of wholeness. He's a scientist considering the facts of a a holy Whole Experiment. He's an artist looking keenly at the sacred. Everything Dickinson's Clown ponders is *tremendous*, or as Dolly Parton says, *beautiful*. I'll take this—a thrilled conviction of being alive, and precious. And vibrational, in song, like the frogs in the pond.

In these days when it is life and death how we see each other and our earth, the Clown is hallowed, an essential worker. "Send in the clowns," the theater world says, when it is chaos on stage and the show must be rescued. The Clown is on the front lines. That is, the artist who *lives deliberately*, engaging with the environment *as if it were their own*. In such gaze, Earth sings.

Driveway Improv for *This Our Life*

My Fellow Mortals are whom I am celebrating with you in this book, the sequel to *Here for the Present*. In that book, I was trying to figure out how to prevent future smacks on the head by seeing where I was going, understanding being *present*—however short-lived—as a gift of consciousness.

Here now are characters on my path that I sing in driveway improv and rest stop flash memoirs of engagements with our world, when this world just comes upon me, manifests in worms and turkeys and breakaway camels and spiders, in wondrous ways like stars to wise men on camels, or angels to the six-year-old William Blake, or worrisome, as Dante found himself facing wild beasts, or glorious, as John Muir experiences the wild world: *The Glory! The Glory!* he pants, on top of some peak I would be afraid to climb (but not you).

I'm not alone in this singing. You are here. You are with me when the hummingbird appears. Vibrating in place, *Your parents*, our son used to say, as we faced these hummingbirds staring at us intently at my parents' house, and I agreed. And now I think it is he, my son, coming back to me from his life in the nebulae, and you agree.

So Much to Tell

You, dear Reader, are Emily Dickinson's March whom I ask to *come right upstairs with me, I have so much to tell*. She is gushing with excitement at March's Spring emergence:

> Dear March—Come in—
> How glad I am—
> I hoped for you before—
> Put down your Hat—
> You must have walked—
> How out of Breath you are—
> Dear March, how are you, and the Rest—
> Did you leave Nature well—
> Oh March, Come right upstairs with me—
> I have so much to tell—

March might be huffing and puffing—"how out of breath you are," but it's Dickinson herself in her thousands of poems who is breathless with "Nature's news." She is bubbling with earthly festivity. "I'll tell you how the sun rose," she says, "a ribbon at a time." What a present! What being present! She is our warbling companion. In our day, Mary Oliver writes *Instructions for Living a Life*: *Pay attention. Be astonished. Tell about it.* (from *Sometimes*). I thought perhaps to title this book in Dickinson's and Dante's honor, *I have so much to tell*, telling you of some Fellow Mortals I have met in this our journey.

We are called to Thoreau's woods in *Walden*, where it's going to be a beautiful day, as in Mr. Rogers' *Neighborhood*. It's dark now, but there's Thoreau's *infinite expectation of dawn*.

And we're upstairs with Emily Dickinson chatting up March. In how wholly and holy she sees the world, isn't it a portrait of Dickinson herself who is the artist writing *A little madness in the Spring*?

I see her Clown, a fellow artist, who has Nature figured out—or rather, humbly, not figured out. It's being floppy-footed and bulb-nosed, tumbling with amazement, humbled, scrambled, succumbed in pondering, that leads to appropriate exuberance on incandescent earth. The Clown knows *he* doesn't own earth. He sees *this tremendous scene* with wonder. *Pondering,* he is thoughtful, reflective, *deliberate*.

The Thoreau takeaway he did not say, but did say: *most men go to the grave with the song still in them*

What he did say is "The mass of men live lives of quiet desperation." He goes to the woods to find a way not to die, not to die without having lived.

The woods that Dante finds himself lost in, Thoreau said he had to go *away* to, to live deliberately, in an *experiment in living*, an *Experiment in Green*, to see what is possible when you ponder.

Perhaps to *ponder* is a way to live deliberately.

In such woods, there are *Cantos: There alway, alway something sings*. (Ralph Waldo Emerson, "Music").

Narrator Cantos

I always wanted to be in the choir. The Choir was for sixth graders of Loma Alta Elementary School in Altadena, California. Finally I was in the sixth grade singing oooo-oooo-oooo-oooo oooo—oooo, *The Night Before Christmas* in a bliss of belonging, belting out a song in one voice in this our life. But I was called out, and told I was going to be The Narrator instead. Now everyone knows I cannot sing, but I love to sing. And so my life has been The Narrator, as teacher, as poet, my own ways of singing to extol what the choir and ariasters and soloists are singing. Dante (Cantos), Robert Burns (Songs), Whitman ("Song of Myself"), Dickinson ("did I sing too loud?"), Emerson ("Music"), Thoreau, Dolly Parton, Ian Chillag, Cameron Awkward-Rich, Robin Wall Kimmerer, Sandra Gilbert, the three Staffords William, Kim, and Guthrie, Bayo Akomolafe, Xochitl Julisa Bermejo, Shondra Buchanan, Amanda Gorman, public intellectual folks and wise guys, poets and philosophers and scientists spanning almost a thousand years. All blend and blur, and we can't tell who's who, exactly, because they are all saying the same thing. Sing! Sing of and to each other, and hear our Fellow Mortals sing themselves. The news is: everything is alive in its own way. Singing.

And so I sing in my own way.

I thought I was living deliberately. Or at least responsibly. The Muse has other ideas.

Although I am committed to telling my own news of Earth's story, fortified with the songs of the scientists and poets, all the wisdom voices that sing it, I ignore my Muse very often, because like you I am busy with Life. And the Muse to me appears as a distraction, an interruption or disruption in an orderly and hard-won plan of the day. You're going about your life, and suddenly, you're jarred. You're hurtling, on schedule, and suddenly you STOP. Maybe it's a turkey at the side of the road, maybe it's a worm on the sidewalk, or maybe it's a sight of a branch against a pale sky. You, by which I mean me, but if Dante and Einstein are right, we're the same, pull over, to a rest stop or off ramp (you can see I am very often in my car in *this our life*). Thoreau said if we don't get into those woods, we will not live at all. We need to go to those woods. Okay, Muse. I'm yours. Here I am, on the page, writing down Cantos.

I think it's when I'm on the path to where I'm going in a busy and serious life I love, with people I love, like you, and I suddenly come to a stop. seeing something beautiful, something mysterious, and I ponder, that I know I am on the right path. I see Fellow Mortals.

So let's say we're humming along with our plans, and then there's the notice of something inside or outside, and we pull over to a rest stop, or sit in the driveway, because as soon as we get out, you know this, it's back to Real Life, and our Work, and there's no responsible time to write it down and ponder and not know and think about it. Pondering requires its own space, its own place, even though it seems off road, unsocial, kooky, making of a car or parking lot an eccentric writer's nook, or loft, or fireside.

Even though the pondering may not appear as a *song*, the kind of writing you think of as a Poem, or Canto, it is a thought that takes place on a page. These meditations on the phenomena I come upon in my day are my woods in which I can find myself and my place in this universe—a beholder, a ponderer. Something alive in its own way, singing, the gift of some kind and quirky Muse, making my day. . . *deliberate.*

I write down these ideas that come so inconveniently, even dangerously. Writing a meditation, a Canto, may seem strange when cars are honking or a driver hurls disrespectful words about your driving style. You may be seen as a Clown, in your pondering. But when you do, the blur of a World as we know it falls away. Life gets into focus. Even muck is beautiful, and it sings.

**Perhaps what I pull over for—
interruptions and disruptions—is wonder.**

And who knows when and where the Muse will come? It's when we're doing something else, on our way, in our day. I was sitting in bleachers with friends waiting for the Pasadena New Year Parade to start, when I grabbed my iPhone to write:

What kind of flower would I be if I could live in such winter sun as this, this January 1 st day in sunshine, under blue sky? What would my roots come up with? Living in those dark hours, but then, hour after hour of this warmth seeping in my veins? What kinds of petals? What colors? Would I be as wild as The Bird of Paradise, or improbably tough as an orchid, intricate as a peony? Ruffle on ruffle in ruffle, delicacy of color. Or the canna lilies. Those veins. What would I become? Because to live in such light, rooted in darkness, surely you would become something beautiful, something infinite, so inspiring to behold, and desirous to be given to someone you love, or to grace a table, or to comfort in a dark room, to sing of light. Surely you would become that thing, that being, that could be of use in this world. Your imagination would root, in such light, and you would flower somehow, someway.

—From my iPhone Notes, written on a bleacher during the Rose Parade in Pasadena, California 2024.

Then the parade began, and I was lost in that joy.

*Kiss the joy as it flies
and you will live in eternity's sunrise*
—Joyce Cary, *The Horse's Mouth*, quoting from William Blake's "Eternity"

These Cantos sing of surrender. I try to let go of the belief that you can know, or say it right. Or always be, in this particular life form. I bow to this reality that we have to let go of everything in a mortal life we all share, with gratitude that, in the words of the brilliant and immortal and moving Louis the Can of Cola, "it is a gift to be anything at all" (Ian Chillag's *Radiotopia*, "Everything Is Alive."). And I cherish the idea—from physics as well as poetry—that we are together in this fated plight, this plighted fate, this plated light.

The Clown is pondering: Dante says *this our life* 700 years before Einstein. And, if e=mc2, then we=each other. It is a case of the Mayan saying, *you are my other me*. The poets always get it first. Then the idea from Robert Burns—the lines that changed the world—that even a lowly pest like a mouse is our *earthly companion*, a *Fellow Mortal*. We each are a Magic Mirror to whomever sees us, wasp or hummingbird or crow, muskrat, partridge, bear or cougar, willow or beech, or for that matter, mountain, rock, our sun, our galaxy, the Local Group: everything is a fellow mortal.

So, from the Clown's reasoning, you'll meet my rooster, and chicken, and koi, squid, and octopus, and a not scary spider and the bad cat Garbo, and a rock, and a river, a worm, my dazzling turkey, and you'll see me at sea in a market losing my blueberries.

And guess what? If we're all each other, then you are right here with me. In each of these encounters in the woods with our Fellow Mortals, each alive singing in its own way, you're in the woods, too. In these Cantos, *you're* now on your path; you are *living deliberately*. You are *pondering*, Emily Dickinson's Clown. A little lost, lonely, not knowing, a requirement for seeing where we are with renewed attention.

To sing about and hear singing of our earth is our common ground. To hear the lowly and almighty— who can tell which is which? It is all a gift, what we share with each other, our cherished journey companions in *this our life*.

To this our life! To the woods! Earth has so much to tell us yet. It's still an experiment. It's still green. Okay, *let's go then, you and I*" ("The Love Song of J. Alfred Prufrock," T.S. Eliot).

I've Got You, Babe
—Sonny and Cher
Oh but you're good to me—Hozier

I'm in the middle of my life (I hope—eighty is closer than sixty). I face those snarling beasts in residence on my path. I live in those dark woods. But I've got my Virgil, Dante, and so many other poets and troubadours . . . sunshine on a cloudy day. I've got you, babe. All the lyrics, soundtracks to this our life.

What keeps us going? What can lift us, against all natural laws of gravity and certain fate? If we are each other, we burrow and fly, we are infinite, every day. We can be lifted by our own notice of things of this world still growing, still green, including even possibly ourselves. And the people who are no longer with us in life, they must be sung; those in my life I have lost I find alive again in these Cantos.

If we think of how Dickinson's Clown sees our earth, as *our own*, we have a stake in how it is seen, what happens to it as a consequence, and this is why I sing in these Cantos of my encounters with this world of ours, this life of ours, to myself, and to you. "You are my sunshine." We sing this at the best of times, around campfires. It's true! Science says. It's you, after all, whom Clown Cantos ponder, you, my sunshine.

And on that note,
with love, your fellow mortal author B

A LITTLE MADNESS IN THE SPRING

ROCK

Fool's Gold

Panning for gold,
this wasn't serious.

I did not plan on it as a poem.

It was a media event.
I was just an observer.

But even parents photographing children had to pay,
I didn't mind, it was worth the thirty-five marks,
how often are you in gold country, so far North?

But once you paid
you were fitted for boots to your knees,
and I was sitting like any investigative reporter
in the middle of a gold river
the color of coffee with cream in the morning light
only a cold, cold river, melted North Pole slush,
on a wet log, holding an icy tin wok,
sloshing rocks and sand and silt through my fingers
in the cold, cold water, feeling glacier's innards,
earth's parts it parts with.

And I began to think about what I was doing,

Henry James' "try to be
one of those on whom nothing is lost,"
lines which come to me in moments like these
when I am suspended in a cave
deep beneath the earth
or in a monsoon in the tropics
fleeing snakes hanging from trees
or, in this case,
sorting out rocks
in a river in the Arctic
while moose and reindeer stroll

and mosquitoes bite me and bite me
in places I did not know I had skin.

I love rocks, why?

Green, gold, black, pink, red, white, clear,
colors of flowers.
Why do I love them,
and why are they the color of flowers?
Or of plaid or polka dots?

The patterns worn by clowns,
patterns I love.

Rocks, once pulsing, liquid,
earth's blood perhaps, from its heart—
now cooled, permanent monuments
to a live earth,
to the creative act.

Why we wear rocks. Yes?
To declare love that is never ending.
Why we seek gold, deep within the earth,
why we want it on our bodies,
part of the shine of the heavens.

I rinse and sort, sloshing my pan
through the water, until I am left
with a black and pink silt forming
river and leaf patterns,
reminding me how all of nature is one.

Now I begin to think of this sloshing as a poem,
not writing one,
but how the process of writing a poem
is panning for gold.
Situating yourself in the muck,
mud, cold water,

sorting through experience,
Painstakingly, systematically, exquisite care,
yet you know you are losing
everything,
it is all going through your fingers,
the river's current is taking it.

You feel and discard,
not knowing
what you are keeping
and what is being lost.

And what it is worth.

Sorting through experience like so many rocks,
feelings, thoughts, memories, ideas, sensations,
the too-big rinsed and discarded,
then smaller and smaller tossed back in the river,
and you are aware of how beautiful they are,
the ones you are throwing away,
their colors, intricacies, complexities
of texture, shape, form, and how interesting:
but you do not keep them.

I rinse and sort, sloshing my pen
through the water, until I am left
with a black ink silt forming
river and leaf mind patterns,
reminding me how all of nature is one.

You finger them, rinse them,
examine them
and throw them back,
because you are looking for—
gold. Something—
heavier, softer, more precious,
harder to come by—
and you sort and sift, in the rain,

bitten by mosquitoes and black flies,
harassed by wasps,
Sweating and wet and cold.

You sort and sift and slosh
until what is in your pan is so fine,
what is in your pen is so fine,
and you try to recognize
in that fine glinting black silt
now clean of all extraneous shape
and form and color and texture,
gold—in dust, as flecks, perhaps a nugget,
that could transform your life,
The nugget you patiently sift for hour after hour
and year after year,
growing old—

Panning not for the poem but what makes the poem,
the gold nugget or flecks added up,
the dull solid matter unquestionably valuable—
the image that will stay and stay
and shine and mean
and change lives forever.

And your fear, that in your sifting and sloshing,
you are throwing away flecks of gold,
that you don't recognize it,
are careless or not skillful enough
in the rinsing, editing process,
that your instinct for gold,
what it is, what it isn't,
is not sure enough,
and you are letting go of the real thing—
you never know this.

You only keep refilling your pan,
and working it over and over again,
the undifferentiated mud of experience,

of living, your rocks and clay,
and you know gold is there
for anyone who can see it
and you know that.

But you forget it
in the simple sitting on a log
sorting through rocks
feeling in fingers
the earth, the earth itself,
and these rocks you let go,
as we pick weeds,
more delicate, more savory,
than roses.

Still, we work for gold,
line after line,
in the muck and mud.

And after a while
everything we see is wet and gold and shining,
And you can't tell what is river, what is sky,
what is blinding mud—see, see
gold outside the pan,
it's all around.

And the wealth you find,
in the pan that is a pen,
it's the happiness you feel,
it's what you get throwing away everything else.
it's yourself in the struggle
thrown away, thrown in,
and in the cold water
you see, you see,
it's gold,
everywhere you look,
all and nothing is gold.

Above Inari, Arctic Circle

SPIDER

In Which I Happily Give Up

To tell you the truth I didn't feel so good
going after a living spider,
a Daddy Long Legs,
whom I believe to be a harmless innocent,
but it is the point,
we can't have spiders.

At the first sign that things are less than shipshape
they move in.
Out of dust balls growing in corners
like a forgotten science class experiment,
suddenly gangliness of knuckly legs
and protruding bellies of spiders,
impervious to pity,
no sense of fair play,
taking advantage of the human distractions of distress.

Pneumonia the least of it.

In spite of my weakened state I rise.
In the ancient ritual going back to the cave,
I reach for a broom.

In fact, a broom is my life dancing pal,
and now the panic tumult in my chest,
heaving breaths,
subside into arcs of rhythm,
the loveliness of back and forth,
what seas must feel
as moon swings them,
as I sway
with my thin-as-a-rail ballroom dance partner,
and already I am feeling better,
when I swipe an enormous Daddy Long Legs
a foot up the wall,
in some aerial acrobatic antigravity Zen pose.

Instead of collapsing into the ball of dust
in a fractal cosmic collision,
the spider appears unscathed.
now two feet across the floor.

I am a surprised Captain Hook
humbled by an aerial Peter Pan,
I am a thousand times its size,
I have the weapon of annihilation,
and I swipe at it again.

It moves, not fast, in its own direction,
away from the broom's stiff fingers.

Again, I plunge the now enormous-seeming broom
into this iota,
this practically nothing of a being,
and again, this object of attack
is not touched
by the broom's bristles.
It moves deftly away.
It walks, unhurried.

I swipe at it again: it is the principle.
The spider moves slowly, erect.

It's the dignity: that's it.

I open the patio door and hold it open
as the spider makes its way.
I wait.
I lean on the broom,
as the spider steps over the transom
like some lunar module,
taking its time,

with such—not fearless,
because that would suggest fear in the first place—
calm faith in its life,
its choice not to tangle with a broom,
not to have a bristled fate of crumple and heap.
I stand aside,
as the spider disappears,
and lives.

Weighing less than a dry leaf,
less matter than a grain of salt,
its flimsy being is majesty.
My broom and I bow
as I brush back and forth a few times
in happy uselessness, in holy reprieve.

CAMEL

Camel Escapes and "Stomps" Man
in Southern California
(The Associated Press, Saturday, February 15, 2014)

When is the last time you thought about a camel? I know, me too. They are not in our lives or even in our dreams. Certainly not our poems. Bears are epic. The fox has a whole anthology. Camels have Kipling making fun of their hump. Camels are an analogy for ugliness (Mary J. Blige). Camels sell cancer. But you don't worry about camels when you set out in the morning, that is for sure.

So I was surprised to read this story, right after a three-year-old choking on a grape (thinking of Blanche Dubois, "I shall die of an unwashed grape")—note to self: avoid grapes, they are "slippery" and "even paramedics could not extract the grape, which slid back into the airway with each breath." A pregnant woman is hit by a snowplow, in the parking lot, loading groceries, having gone to an OB-GYN appointment, and dies—note to self, avoid parking lots in snowstorm; avoid groceries in general; avoid appointments.

If you are like me, the news is a cautionary tale. So I take careful note. Setting forth, snacking at the table, even parking, can get you in lethal trouble. But these are hazards of everyday morning life. On the other hand, consider this: a camel "escaped from an enclosure in a Southern California high desert community Friday" and "stomped a 72-year-old man who tried to capture it."

Well now. A camel who only exists in our imaginations perhaps as exotic transportation of the Three Wise Men, or perhaps in history, Napoleon, or the Arab king Gindibu, in the battle of Qarqar in 853 BC, or as readers of Xenophon know, from the Battle of Thymbra in 547 BC, with Cyrus the Great of Persia and Croesus of Lydia. (Apparently horses go berserk at camels' smell; thus camels were used as scent weapons to make havoc with equestrian sensibilities.) Oh, yes, Lawrence of Arabia—Peter O'Toole got the part because Marlon Brando "did not want to spend two years on a camel." So the point is, camels are in our minds as history and legend and not in our Friday morning in Palmdale.

My father, who served with the British fighting Rommel the Desert Fox in World War II, told me that camels were the worst. I do remember that now.

Camels are mean, he said. They will spit at you, and it is personal. He was a forward observer in Tunisia and blown up in a mine across enemy lines and dragged himself five miles back to his troops and was in the hospital over a year, and met Eleanor Roosevelt, and now that I recall, all that he would say about the whole experience was that camels are mean.

So camels might be in family history even. Albeit long ago and far away. But see here. The camel was reported chasing cars "shortly after 8:30 am. . . . 'My dad . . .tried to catch it, and it must have cornered him or something, and it took off after him, bit him on the head and knocked him down and stomped on him,' Skylar Dossenback said." Her father needed stitches. He remains in the hospital.

"A neighbor came out and saw the commotion and got the camel away from him. . . And the camel actually started chasing them, and they had to jump in a car, and the camel was running around after everybody."

This is fine news. You are driving, listening to NPR or Travis Tritt, "It's a great day to be alive," and just got a Starbucks coffee. You drive in your lane, and it's stoplights, some horns, some trucks. And then calomp calomp, something furry, something huge is in your driver-side mirror, as you wait at the signal, wait, its head—not a horse—

Coming at you, 40 miles an hour, it does not run, only speeds up, seven feet high thousand pounds of humps and hair and something hanging from his mouth, is some ancient farfalle. As you furiously google, what is coming at me, as you ask Siri, you are led to 10 Amazing Facts About Camels. You pause at No. 8:

8. Camels mate all year round, but they have a favorable period when vegetation is lush. The male is extremely aggressive during mating period (he can bite by the foot his rider). During the arousal, he shows off his teeth, salivate abundantly, and the epidermic glands of the neck and shoulders are extremely active. He urinates frequently, and keeps the head and the fore limbs as raised as possible. Males possess an organ called dulla, like a pink bladder, normally harbored in the throat. During the rut period, the male throws the dulla out of his mouth in a display dominance. Dulla hangs like an inflated pink tongue and at the same time the male burbles, a disgusting sight to most humans.

Male combats for females can be deadly, due to the sharp teeth and to the mouth with the largest opening amongst all ruminants (the male can grab in the mouth the head or the neck of his adversary). The Jacobson organ from the <u>roof</u> of the mouth is employed by the male (like in many mammals, a behavior called flehmen) to assess through urine hormones if the female is receptive (ovulating) or not. If the female is receptive, mating occurs on the place. Camels mate laying on the ground! (in decubitus position). Camels and lamas are the only mammals employing this position for mating. Mating lasts 10-20 minutes, and is extremely noisy, the male making a call like "duloo".

You do not know if the noise you hear is duloo or burbling. You are too thrilled to be disgusted. This was not on your worry list today, a car chase by a bonkers camel hungry for a knock-down drag-out fight, and no pity for the elderly. By something with more than one stomach with a scent that freaks out stallions. With a third transparent eye and nostrils that zip, who can drink 40 gallons in 3 minutes and wait to pee a month. Something like that.

A google search turns up the news that the camel is owned by A-List, a company that trains animals for films. Trainer1234 blogs, *His name is Wally and he is generally very sweet. He was most likely terrified to be out of his pen which never happens for him.* So what we are left with, our takeaway today—ER doctors extract the grape. They deliver the baby. They stitch the man's face. And the military it says right here strives to make a pizza that lasts for years (I know that even ones we get today last at least a week and taste just fine, hot or cold). The good news is you just never know. The things you think you know, the ER can help.

ROOSTER

To All We Secretly Love

At that time they say that the Emperor Honorius in Ravenna received the message from one of the eunuchs, evidently a keeper of the poultry, that Roma had perished. And he cried out and said, "And yet it has just eaten from my hands!" For he had a very large cockerel, Roma by name; and the eunuch comprehending his words said that it was the city of Roma which had perished at the hands of Alaric, and the emperor with a sigh of relief answered quickly: "But I thought that my fowl Roma had perished." — Procopius, The Vandalic War (De Bellis III.2.25–26), circa 532

If you have ever heard a rooster crow, pronounce morning, a throaty pounce on light, you might not be surprised at how beloved Roma was to the emperor, who doted on the feathered feisty spirit.

If you have ever shouted out the kitchen door, *ducks and chickens!*, to come get spaghetti and salad, and seen them surge.

If you have ever thought you had chickens until early one morning in Pasadena there is the cry of a rooster, and it's not a metaphoric Thoreau Chanticleer, it's not Chaucerian, it's an actual rooster going cock-a-doodle-do, or er-er-er-er-er!

And you wake up laughing that there is such a sound in your world, even though your neighbor calls the police and you are told to get rid of the rooster, as the neighborhood is not zoned for rooster crow. But now you know it is a magical place, or, better, a real place after all.

If you have ever held a rooster, all squirmy glossy feathers, indignant and staring, spurs and crest and scorpion tsunami tail, its fervent red and green and blue from gulped darkness, pecked star, you may begin to understand what he meant, the emperor, his relief that it was not his young rooster but Rome that had fallen.

You may begin to understand why the Portuguese describe a legend: "Ah, but you have been accused and sentenced to death, and I can't change the sentence on just your word without proof. How do you think you can prove your innocence, my good man?" "But Sir, I swear that I am innocent," the man insisted. . . His eyes fell on a servant carrying in a large platter of fowl, steaming with seasonings. He fell to his knees. "Lord God," he prayed, "as Peter, your servant, denied you at the cock's crow, would that you show my innocence as your humble servant by this rooster's crow…" so he said "If I am innocent, this rooster will crow three times." All eyes turned to the platter of steaming cooked fowl and widened in wonder and amazement as the rooster got up, ruffled his feathers and crowed loudly. "The Lord has indeed spoken," the Judge said in awe, and rising to his feet, he proclaimed, "The rooster, henceforth, shall be a reminder to us and to our children after us, of this, the Lord's message. So shall it be in our land forever!"

You can see why the country of France, for example, should adopt the rooster as a symbol of classical civility. You can see why Sydney would name its rugby team the Roosters.

When Grandma comes to visit, and it is time to kill the old red rooster, it's missing. So is Thessus. Aha!

The dinner is turnips and potatoes and chess pie.

Later, Thessus is found by the creek, holding rooster matching the colors of water, colors of sunrise. No one is mad. Everyone loves the loyal roo, who would fight to the death to protect his own.

But the reason why is his leafy feathers the colors of gorgeousness.

His principled clawed stand.

His peevish pecking.

His notice of morning that does not get by him, even when it sneaks in gray: he is alive to its colors of rooster.

BLUEBERRY

I Forgive Gravity

Shake a mass and the change in the **gravitational** field —
the **gravitational** wave — propagates at that same **speed**. "So the fact that
the **speed of gravitational** waves is equal to the **speed** of electromagnetic
waves is simply because they both travel at the **speed** of information,"
Creighton says.(the result of google search, *the speed of gravity*)

It is not that I am so old, to look at—it's true I have Nellie's song, "I'm as normal as blueberry pie" from *South Pacific* on my mind this morning (if you even remember) but can you tell? I don't know what it is about me, exactly, that spells feeble. But in the supermarket, I drop a box of blueberries—of course, of course, and blueberries—as one does, as they do, take on a life of their own, leaping the box, free now, at last, to wander, as was in them all along to do. And not just wander—like the bears who love them, and amble amiably among the shrubs, they are fast. Look at them now, suddenly scattered under the freezer doors, down the aisles with chips and vinegar and still moving. They are a sprawl worthy of Los Angeles, of Rio, of Mexico City, of Shanghai and Dhaka, moving with inexorable speed, outwards, across linoleum that invisibly slopes, demonstrating curved space scientists proclaim. It is the Big Bang before our eyes, theory in motion, cosmic expansion, commotion in a teacup—or, as in this case, a market. Gravity at work—blueberries spreading out at the speed of light, and it's true, it's true.

All right. I've got my hands full, because I did not take a cart (Fool!) thinking I was only coming to get—what was it—wait. Now I'm holding two baskets of berries, a mango, a dozen brown eggs, lemon yogurt, and ice cream, clearly the tipping point, as I adjust my items and the blueberries escape their corrugated cardboard nests, experimenting with flying (as they saw the birds and butterflies alighting on them in their bush lives), and landing (as they saw the herons), and the swoop move perfected by the osprey on the pond next to their home. The trick is to land without being mushed, so that they can roll, and roll, and roll.

A quart of blueberries does not sound like so much, in the greater scheme of things, not a galaxy with a billion or so stars, but right now, it is a lot. The berries' arcs expand, outward, outward. I have to pick them up before they are squashed and transform shoppers into a classic comedy sketch, men in long-coat tuxedos and top hats, strolling in oblivious snobbery until they are upended

by a banana peel, to the delight of passersby (why is comedy heartless?). The supermarket is not an audition stage for aspiring slapstick, and more to the point, tragedy or at least misfortune of the unsuspecting (a quick trip to the store for milk and coffee filters, calling one's partner from the ER with the news that breakfast will be delayed).

I lean over and a man—I tell you, he was way older than I, in a suit, for some reason, crouches and starts picking them up, and handing them to me, and then a woman in overalls and pigtails and tattoos, and then a young man in running shorts, and then a lady in a hat, stout and stiff, but bending down, and I can't keep track, people are chasing down blueberries, as I stand with my cardboard collecting box, a rickety center of this physics of common love, blueberries and people alike going the distance. Orbited by young and old, I'm a sun of sorts, or a hive homing in with honeyed news of this world, and I'm saying, O Thank you! Thank you!

And here's the thing, none of us in this endeavor, and it is a joint endeavor, a community in action, knows who each other is, whom we vote for, whom we root for, and who knows, maybe if we knew we would hate each other and wish each other off the planet. But scratch us, let a blueberry fall. Let loose a disorganized old lady, and see laws of the universe reveal the human spirit, its truths at speed of light.

LAKE

Washing the Lake

I'll wash the dishes, I say.
It's nothing more than gesture,
the politeness of a guest at the end of the day.
It's my hands—
I can't stand to stir them in water.
But my hosts don't understand.
Then it turns out there is no dishwasher.
There is a cove.
I am handed a bucket,
and pointed in the direction of the dock.

Now, washing the dishes,
it is wonderful before I realize it,
even before I think it is a poem.

Not the poem that comes to me,
but the poem I need to write.
The poem I wait for, do not even seek—
ready as when you reach
for the camera when you see a certain scene,
to capture something you already know, or more.
A poem is not to record but to explore.

It is the map we end up with, yes,
but the poem is also the reason for the journey,
why we ever took off from what we know.
We think we do not know enough,
we become restless,
we give up a known world.

The poem is our interpreter,
telling us what we have seen,
our guide, keeping us alive
in terrain we thought we knew.
It shows us how to know
what we know.

Standing in twilight, a lake of light,
the two-fold wrinkled light
of day and night, sky's shiny flabby folds,
my hands and wrists
in sauna-warmed rust-colored lake water and suds,
feeling glasses slippery as eels skid
from my tremulous touch,
tracing their rims and sides
as smooth as ice,
as ripe melon when you are scooping out the seeds.

I look at the lake:
I think, it is the lake whose edges I am tracing,
its contours, insides, bottom and sides;
suds and ripples in the sunlight, they are one,
and my hands feel reeds and birches, clouds and frogs.

The surface I see is not flat,
no, it resembles something insubstantial,
like clouds appear, something that isn't even there,
not even to see.

It's the light now, it makes the water seem opaque,
shimmer but not ripple or break,
like the definition of matter,
nothing solid about it.
Nothing could float on it.

I am staring so hard.
The problem is there is nothing to see
but reflection, as lake appears nothing but sky.

Trying to find words for what I see,
but the words don't come.
This is like—what? I wonder.
Poems need analogies,
but what I see does not need anything.
People need analogies.

The clouds, so white and expressive,
define the Finnish blue—
well, what is the verb for what clouds do?

This landscape defeats me,
when I try to understand it in words.
A lake at twilight, and not just a lake,
but washing dishes,
as if I am washing the lake itself.

Never mind the poem,
I am enjoying washing the dishes,
right here and now.
Sometimes just the facts are enough,
more than enough.

I am washing dishes, and I think
this is significant.
This matters.

Washing the dishes outside here is a restoring of order,
sensuous exploring of surface,
shimmer of glitter and shine and suds.

My hands emerge with fork or cup.
How many women have stood here so,
By some lake or river or sea,
Scrubbing the bowl that held porridge?
This is Egypt, this is Maine,
This is History, this is Keats' Truth and Beauty.

I dip my fingers in cold rinse water.
I am happy.
I take my time.

I am sorry when the dishes are dripping and clean,
spread out on the table,
bowls, plates, cups, glasses and spoons.

Of all the things they hold,
this is what I want most.
The happiness of my hands
in lake water.

COW

This is the Day the Lord Has Made:
Do You Pass Up Heaven on Earth?

Cows laze in the winter sun. Oh, this looks like a pastoral scene. But it's not a painting. I'm on I-5, its flat stretch of fields. Then I realize I'm looking at a corral, and I see the big shed.

Ah, their end is clear. But they do not seem upset and why not. A hammer to the head, really, is this so bad a way to go? Or a shot, a blinding flash and hot burn and heaven. Or whack. Thud. It's over.

Like they said on NPR Car Talk through Grant's Pass. I want to be fat said his third father-in-law. That way I die of a heart attack and it's over. Boom. No family worrying or grief. The joggers who watch their weight they end up in the hospital dying of nothing. They have no disease. They're just dying. And it takes forever. The family is going crazy. No thanks. I'll stay a big guy.

I can see this I think, as I come to Heaven on Earth. Their free pieces of cookies and berry pie. Their six-inch cakes. Their one-pound cinnamon rolls. I'm munching on a bag of wilted spinach leaves I could not bear to throw out, and also my mother would say when we are thirsty, drink lettuce. Yes, she drank lettuce and died of nothing over three years.

Yet on the phone with my sister, I'm passing Heaven on Earth. She says: personally, I would have thrown out the spinach, freed the cows, eaten the cake/pie/cookies and have thrown *in* a diet coke!

What is this life of renunciations, to not get big like the man who says "I'll stay a big guy," so he can die wham like that and not put himself and everyone else into the shenanigans of grief. Maybe I will decide not to opt for the smaller life. I may live a big life yet and die right.

I think of these cows along I-5. When I go, I want it to be tha-wang. I want to live right. Freed. I want to die of a big life.

Commentary:

I-5 High Five! I wrote in a rest stop on I-5 (CA) north of Willows and the 505 turn off, under the eucalyptus trees. I remember the sun, orange gold, through the leaves—it was low on the horizon, about a half hour of daylight to go. In the rolling hills pastoral there were cows lying peacefully in grass by the road, and I was struck by the incongruity of their idyll in the face of their certain slaughter, probably immanent—and then, why not? Indeed! A way to go . . . At the time I didn't end the flash memoir—I thought. I had a larger whole of the experience in my mind when I started writing on the Notepad on my iPhone, but Sophia got back in the car from the rest stop, and we proceeded driving to get as far as we could in daylight.

But it seems that to leave it off like that, *I want to die of a big life*, maybe that is right. The poem leaves me as I ponder my decision to live right, so called, without the cakes and pies, my Heaven on Earth—in this case, to decide not to forgo Heaven on Earth, to do what we were meant to do in the day, rejoice, and be glad in it. (Psalm 118:24)

BEAR

Night Hunger, Wild Hunger

I

The last thing my father says to me as I fold myself into a sleeping bag like an egg white meringue into plaid batter, and he zips the stars, leaving me to a canvas darkness far far darker than the night, is what to do in case of a bear.

II

This is not at all what I was worried about. I have worries. So do you. We know none of us leads a sensible life. I know what a sensible life is, I just do not live it. I need a vacation, in nature, yes, but, a national park, with my parents, greeting me, Now honey, no phones are going to ring, you can write all day, and no one's going to be mean to you.

Now: bears.

III

Yes, he says, bears, they forage for food at night. They cause, and he pauses, quite a lot of trouble. Yes, I remember now, seeing the trees with poems nailed to them, a forest of signs, but the yellow metal messages I thought I had time to read later are telegrams to be read at once, Federal Law: Lock Up Your Food. Violators will have food confiscated and be subject to a fine. The rangers have a meeting and advise: If a bear should approach, scare it away. Make an angry noise. Be belligerent. Holler. Yell. Grunt. Bears understand this kind of language. They leave.

Suddenly life is simple. You are scared of bears.

From my journal.

I didn't sleep well. Daddy said to make sure no food was in the tent for the bears—and if one came in, to yell, angrily—and I lay awake for hours, trying to think of what in the tent was edible to a hungry bear, and then the expression, **hungry as a bear** *came to me, and I sat straight up, thinking of a wild bear's hunger, for marshmallows and* *cookies—-of his red eyes, of his claws, tearing at the tent, I thought of what would seem tasty to a bear—the cough medicine, the aspirin, the deodorant—Blue Grass!—the lotion on my lips—making a mental inventory of everything tasty about me—you never think of yourself as tasty—suddenly I realized I could be . . . delicious—I was seized with a powerful sense of the bear's need—I held a pot in my left hand, and clutched a flat fork in my right, to clang the pot when he appeared at the tent's zipper, snorting, wild-eyed with need of marshmallow.*

I held this pan and fork all night, listening for someone walking without shoes.

The next morning, I am groggy and obsessed. Spilled milk on the campsite's wooden table makes me tremble, my son spilling tuna out of his sandwich (don't you realize bears LOVE fish, I scream). He looks at me. I scan the camp with a bear's gleam, what's here for me?

My mother tells me, *Darling* (in her New York accent), *You're not going to have an encounter with a bear*, (an encountah-with-a-bea-ay-uh), *I assure you. You will be lucky to see a bear.* I examine the table next to the tent where we prepare our food. Triscuits: I practice Lamaze breathing to keep myself from passing out. Getting ready for bed, I ask Nicolino for a pot to bang. He brings me a cast-iron frying pan, drops it on my right elbow, the one I injured in Budapest in the taxicab last month, and I cry. He looks at me. My parents are bewildered, *we don't believe this*!

IV

It is night again, the time I have dreaded, when I must go to the tent. I inspect it again, to make sure, to make sure, nothing edible is there. I go through the suitcases, pulling out each T-shirt, sock, pair of pants, knowing it is crazy. In a pocket of Nicolino's pants, I find a Gummy Bear. We have been sleeping with Gummy Bears, a sweet-toothed bear's likeness. Panting, I take out all the clothes, again, one by one, turning out all the pockets. What else is lurking which will lure this bear to my tent?

V

I see this bear, his hunger, which makes him paw into windshields, cross meadows lit with white moonlight, with those red eyes, shake RV's down for something sweet, mangle for sweetness. . . This desire, which makes him maul, tear people from sleeping bags, so cross, so desperate, this sullen panting childish furry beast. This is no children's story. This is a nightmare.

VI

The next day, my son steps on horse manure my Sicilian mother says is good luck, because she wants to see a bear. I am compromised. Want not to see a bear yet want my son to have his wish, to have what he desires, I believe in desire. Is that why I believe in this bear?

VII

This morning my father spots a rush of brown outside the trailer. My mother is ecstatic. She wants to see a bear, too. She and my little boy rush outside together to see this bear, knocking into each other, they run through the pine needles. It is a raccoon. A big raccoon. But they are disappointed. I try to understand this. Clearly the bear they want to see is just something wonderful, like a firefly, some furry emblem of wilderness, a presence that will make the trees and stars authentic. The bear I don't want to see the bear who searches for me even now as I lie here in darkness clutching my pan listening for shuffling and grunts is hunger, is desire, is terrible. It wants to tear people from sleeping bags, it wants to know, what does it mean to sleep, what are we, what does it all mean, as if ripping zippers, crashing windows, crumpling metal doors, overturning ice chests, marauding, would uncover secrets like worms beneath the stones, knowledge it needs now, now. . . It wants to know. It wants to know everything.

VIII

I lie awake, waiting. It knows just where to find me. It's not just that you have the marshmallows and Oreos it craves, perhaps you do and have locked them in an aluminum chest. It's your dreams. It can tell. It can smell the sweetness of your memory, yes, images as crusty and short as croissants, warm with orange marmalade, and slippery with butter and raspberry jam, but more, your desire, it is drawn by the speckly Merced in you, glacially alive with trout swerving, its browns and golds and greens shimmering like ripples over pebbles in your mind. Your desires glitter, catch the bear's quick eye, and the bear cuffs through to memory trout holding their own, ripples in your heart.

IX

Through the bear's violent nuisance we sleep, its vandalizing as it roams, wanting, wanting what is inside—locks, doors, zippers, snaps, these things we think keep things out, keep things closed: bears don't know the difference between side and top, locked door and walls, skin and clothes, it's all the package meant to be unwrapped.

How foolish to think, as I have thought these past nights, of the bear, pausing at the tent flap, imagining the bear unzipping with padded fingers, long claws, delicately grasping the zipper prong, only enough to swivel its monstrous head with its red eyes, to peer into the tent to see what's tasty tonight, to find me, huddled in the corner, waiting with my pot, ready to clang, to shout, to rush out

—when this bear, this bear, could open the tent without using the zipper, could walk in without any flap. Just a rip and suddenly brightness a set of brightness of stars and eyes and perhaps moon, a growl, and an immediate smell in my tent cave, fur against stars. To think of its surprise, its fear, as it leaves me, clutching my pan.

X

Yes—yes—I want to see it—stooped and fat and fast coming round to see me, poking its head in, its huge head at the zipper, its paw pulling wide the tent flaps—I will clank the pans I clutch, I will drive it away in terror, in both of our terror—wondering—me—what I have, what is marshmallow in my blood, brain, desire, memory, all, all I see, all I feel, when this bear comes—

It's out there now, it knows just where to find me.

XI

I believe in this bear.

This bear might kill me if I don't have what it needs, but I know my mother was right, I would be lucky to see this bear. Ah, bear, I wait, ready to be quiet, if you come.

XII

<u>From my journal, November 5, Hilton Hotel, New York City, at the American Studies Conference, five o'clock in the morning, squatting on the red-carpeted staircase in the lobby:</u>

I, I am the bear.

I don't know quite what this means, now, here. Months have passed. It is night still and people are sleeping. I don't understand so many things, I cannot sleep— this night hunger, wild hunger, my room useless, intolerable, room service has nothing to bring me, nothing I need. Worries and darkness and pockets turned inside out— this ice chest shakes, tears open—is it hope? Think of such hope!

GREAT BLUE HERON

Quantum Happiness at Charlie's Boathouse

Tracing quantum curveballs is counterintuitive by nature with concepts like fermions, bosons, spins, spooky entanglement, and particle-wave duality. So, let's go step-by-step to understand them and the study's insights. The ballgame revolves around fermion pairs. Fermions can be subatomic particles or whole atoms. In this case, the physicists modeled using atoms.

The term fermion refers to quantum-statistical properties that the particle has as opposed to the properties of its counterpart particle called a boson, in particular the particle's spin, which is called half-integer for fermions and full-integer for bosons. (These spins aren't exactly like those on a ball. For more, see: Fermions and Bosons for Dummies.)—*Science Daily*

>In the soft blue bright hazy light on a late summer day,
>late in the day,
>sitting on the swing at Charlie's Boathouse,
>is Margaret,
>Blue Heron in residence.
>OK, no one knows if she's a girl,
>she's the one you can count on to be there
>on the days you are lucky.
>You can't count on anything and that's why we name,
>claim unclaimable facts about the universe
>and pretend there is a science in what we can see
>and when it is there
>and what it means when we actually see it.

Glory Is Too Much

>Our Margaret, she's standing,
>at first in profile in the posture
>she posed for in the bird-spotting book.
>It's a hunched-over, dowager scrunched up look,
>a little unkempt, too,
>sort of toad-like, all bunched in the middle,

then this head jutting out sort of peaky.
And then she unfolds from her crouch,
it's that sudden,
and it is grace,
the long leaning extension of her neck peering out,
ending in a beak resulting in a point,
a kind of Leaning Tower of Pisa look,
sleekly balanced, geometrically angled,
perfectly poised.

She stands,
stands while my heart takes in the scene
like a child falling in a field of wildflowers after rain,
grasping them in fisted delight at the capture of something
so wonderful in the hands.
A picture you snap again and again as you stay with it,
your happiness at seeing this sight,
this sighting.

And then, before you know it,
you had nothing to do with it,
you were happy,
you needed nothing more,
the bird—no longer Margaret, I am humbly corrected,
lifts off,
her feet folded back,
flies before your eyes,
her feet extended out as sleekly as her smooth neck,
one long line,
defining sky,
low across the water, flapping,
her flaps against the perfectly still legs and body held aloft,
no movable parts at all in that long extension,
perfectly engineered legs out straight,
as she so slowly,
so balanced, gravity is not at work here,
lands, and stands once again.

Well! I am beyond satisfied.
I see it, but how did it happen?
Sleight of hand.
And then, no!
Another heron, flying perpendicular to the water,
lands.
And there comes another.
Now it is a new proposition altogether.
This is not any longer the kind of wistful sense
of heron as pet we get with a name,
demystifying what always is so far away,
so improbable in our daily vision.

I was so grateful for one.
Now it is beyond the rules for what I need to see,
what I came for,
I am in way over my depth.
Now it is glory,
and glory is always humbling,
glory is multiple, numerous, a quantity.
Hovering on the edge of too much.

And then a white crane flies and lands,
stands there in white long-necked peering perfection.
And another. And another.
There is nothing I can do with words now to do justice to this scene.

Nothing Adds Up

It is science. I count, one, two, three,
one two three, four, amazing quantity,
and what my mind is thinking is,
there are three blue herons,
there are three cranes, now five cranes,
three standing, four flying, one flying,
three standing, nothing adds up,
it is all there at once.

The inaccuracy of the heart's computations,
quantifying happiness.
Happiness is quantum.
The only thing I can do to state my state of thrill,
enumerate a category of wonder,
count as if a number says it all,
more than I can ever say.
The Count on Sesame Street. King Midas.
The king in the counting house in Song of Six Pence.

When it gets right down to it,
our great brains,
our exquisite capacity to recognize Truth and Beauty,
to compute wonder and behold,
our complex minds of science and artistry to comprehend,
respond, are at square one: one, two, three.
The beginning of intelligence,
seeing pattern, this is like that,
they belong, are more than one,
they are different than everything else around them.
We differentiate.
We see.
All that's left is elementary,
what matters,
what we begin with, one, two, three,
the engineered universe,
laws of nature,
and all experience is facts you can count.

Wave and Particle

Sitting on the wooden swing at Charlie's Boat House
as the sun goes about a leisurely plump orange

setting down purples on soft blue hills
like a parent gathers soft blanket around a child's shoulders
setting down soft purples and oranges on gray blue water
rippled as feathers, sleek in places as neck stretched taut,
happiness is easy and I can talk about it fine,
one, two, three, four, five.
Grateful, witness,
I count what never and always can be counted on,
beyond any names,
any words we could have for them,
whenever they appear, just in time,
summoned by our hopes we did not know we had,
by our need for what is totally unexpected—
but why after all we show up
at a blue lake in late afternoon late summer.

IS WHOLESOME EVEN FOR THE KING -

CRANE

When I Think of You I Remember the Cranes in the Helsinki Zoo
For Mr. B

How we stood in the cold and snow. And what has that to do with your warm embrace? How your shoulders expand immense wings to shelter me; how you gather me into you on cold lost nights; some memory of that, as we stand on ice in the blowing snow.

Somewhere in our past you must have been Zeus—surely I have seen this in your thighs—and I the maiden Leda of Yeats' vision of her taken by the god as bird, who took you trusting into my lap, stroking your soft neck, in love with you, beckoning you to me.

And then you stood before me, unfurled, majestic in your wingspan, this was serious and powerful, now, and I was on my own, in a new world. We never hear what Leda thought, and I have never wondered until now.

But the cranes dancing before us awakened my memory of that earlier time and that ancient and eternal life we shared, when you were both God and flew, in our Greek days by dry fragrant mountain valleys above the sea. And now I remember when you were the bird and I was your Nils, and you flew me over mountains and hills, through clouds, above shining winding rivers of white and pale green waters and jagged rocks.

And in the wingspan of the dancing crane, delicate pencil legs lifted to hop and skip, I remember happiness in your embrace; I think of the surprise in you, when you break out, sudden spring bouts of, bursts of, gestures of inexplicable and graceful moments, where you bravely stand and face me, and unfurl your wings; stand before me, and, stately, lift your foot and begin to hop, and flap, for me.

And once again, I am Leda, I am Nils, we are flying, and my hair is in the blowing wind, it is wild, once again, how you like me, how you have always seen in me a wild heart, and you rise dancing and glorious, glorious and dancing, out of my dreams, as old as the hills.

When I think of you, I remember the cranes in the Helsinki Zoo. We stood on a cold and blowy day. What I thought was an accident or miracle, they were undaunted in their joy, they were intent on dancing, wings unfurled, legs lifted, soaring, such flapping happiness, my heart clapped. It was not the cold that took my breath away. It was seeing males jump and leap, to express a fluttery excitement that can't be expressed with your feet on the ground; you have to lift your feet, bend your knees, crook your arms, shrug your shoulders, unfurl your great shoulders.

And I think of these shoulders that shelter me at night, that draw me into them, to be warm and moist. I sleep under wings, under feathers, we nest. When someone would look at me it would look like I am lying, lying under your strong muscular wings; but when I think of you, and me, in your wings, I am flying, we are flying.

LION

In that same time, more than 15,000 people were killed by lightning; 4,000 by bees; 10,000 by deer; 1,300 by rattlesnakes.

SOME FACTS ABOUT MOUNTAIN LIONS

Even though half of California is prime mountain lion country, these animals are rarely seen by humans. In general, mountain lions are calm, quiet and elusive. They are most commonly found in areas with plentiful prey such as deer, bighorn sheep, raccoons, rodents, and other small animals. They usually hunt alone, at night. They typically cover the carcass with leaves or branches and may return to feed on it for several days. Though they are most active at dusk and dawn, they can be seen at any time of the day. Mountain lions are solitary except during mating.

It is due to their secretive and solitary nature that it is possible for humans to live in mountain lion country without ever seeing a mountain lion. The potential for a human to be killed or injured by a mountain lion is quite low compared to other natural hazards. It is more likely that a person will be struck by lightning, for example, than of being attacked by a mountain lion. Over the past 100 years, records show that only 13 fatal mountain lion attacks occurred on the entire North American continent. In that same time, more than 15,000 people were killed by lightning; 4,000 by bees; 10,000 by deer; 1,300 by rattlesnakes.—Brochure at Visitor's Center, Garland Regional Park, Carmel Valley, California

Wilderness n. savage, ferocious, frenzy, insane (Webster's *Dictionary*)

To know you is to know the danger of the heart. Its range: *Secretive, solitary, calm, elusive*. How it is possible to live with someone without ever seeing them.

We live with mountain lions, it is said, and it is safer than lightning (my terror at which you scoff), and you, you love lightning. You love storm, its shattering sounds of wind giving itself utterly to its impulse of velocity, of pent up energies from its time as star, as light. (As I imagine the lion leaping, although I do not know yet from what source is its spring.) You love the bolt, the flash, the universe breaking apart, a crack into the light that is there behind and beyond any darkness in our sights.

It is said that living with lions is safer than life with bees. And you love the honey, the sweetness, you love the hum of bees, their presence meaning that something is near that you love, something growing, fragrant, and thinking of this you hum, too, and sometimes, if someone nears your wings, interrupts your dance, your secret way of knowing where the good things are you might sting—a way of lightning and leap, a way of wind. Rattlesnakes, of course: their sinewy paths, like the river you love to see meander through the marsh grass knowing a heron is nearby and bass below.

And deer: you love the mystery of these creatures that stand so straight and so still, carefully stepping, eyeing everything, knowing without looking what is there. The deer don't care. Without seeming to look: their peripheral vision.

The things you love that frighten and kill, the things you love, still. You behold the lightning and you are thrilled to see the snake. The sound of bees, and the quiet of deer, are worship, and you say you want to see the lion, your own way of prayer. You go at dusk with your faith the lion will appear to you.

All right then. I unhinge my own prayer for safety, I lift off the leather tie on the corral gate of my fears, I let in the knowledge of a startling universe with energy to spare, or, perhaps, let out the knowledge—let it spring, let it kick, let it burn, let it sting.

As dangerous as it seems, this world, loved by a man who loves living with lions, and me, too, me, loved by this man who loves danger, I let go the value of safety, and I say roam and wander and love everything that is wild and free, the way I know that you love me. The way, mortal risk aside, I give my heart to you. Of course, I would not live any other way, for the sighting of you! You, in my wildest dreams.

LOG

Terra Incognita

I lie next to you waiting like a continent with my native tongues and traditions, climates and ways to be discovered.

What leads to discovery?

If you already know something is there, then it's Expedition, Exploration, packing, and planning.

Discovery comes about because, not that there was a hunger, since you did not even know there was this way to satisfy that longing or need—there was a compass, precisely because you did not want to discover, you wanted to keep within the bounds, no, before that, you didn't need a compass, you had a star and a ship, before that a boat, before that, a raft, and for that you only needed a sail, no, only wind, but no, to begin with, just the current could take you, so all you needed was to get in that craft, but what would it take to get you in that scooped out log, what would possess you to leave the shore behind, see your hill and tree get smaller and smaller and disappear?

Why did you ever hollow out that log on the beach, drag it past the banks, what made you even think of a way to harass, or is it caress, water? Was it the duck, that you saw fly, then float?

What did the birds do that made you want to rise and see the secret that makes them sing?

And who knows what you would bring, once you came to me, how I would change, in your naming, what would happen to my donkeys knowing what I know of history: do I want to be on a map?

But what is the purpose then of my waterfalls, my peaks and valleys and little flowers and nice days? So I lie here for you to find me, I wait, I know you've set off, with your compass that only takes you so far, wind will do the rest, and a current that cannot keep you away, you are on your way now, any day your sails will arrive, your exhausted body will sleep on my sands, and when you open your eyes, your soul, still fresh and new, is ready for surprise, good news, my eyes.

The life you came for.

SQUIRREL / FOX

Resurrection Shenanigans

On the sighting by scientists of fox thought extinct, caught by remote cameras leaping orangely in the manner of e.e. cummings' trees *leaping greenly*

i who have died am alive again today—e.e. cummings
Be like the fox: Practice resurrection—Wendell Berry
Shaking it over here, boss!—"Cool Hand Luke"

I praise gods fox can read because what the poets say may help.
Fox and us, if there's a difference, their resurrection and our redemption.

Trees are poems the earth writes.
Of course, says Fox, all insouciance,
the first Forest Professor, holding the Alpine Chair.
He loves Kahlil Gibran.

Why, asks the fox, using the Socratic Method,
the one he taught Socrates in the Grove,
do you think there is such excitement
in the sight of me,
leaping once again on the high slopes?
It was blurred,
but I heard a scientist wept at the photograph.

Yes, squirrel? (I'll have you for breakfast later.)

The squirrel rises to the occasion,
cannot help being a good student,
even though it costs him his life.

Well, from the Buddhist perspective, adds the fox,
life here, life there, it's all flow.
You'll be grass, or me, tomorrow.

You'll live again, just as I have,
despite (you endure this too)

human hunters and hungers,
the quest of skins and tails and stew,
charging forests with knives and nets and guns,
as if our forests were an enemy camp
and the trees, abiding wild life, aided and abetted,
and guilty as charged,
we saw them hung.

People danced on their stumps, left them to rot,
like carcasses of buffalos slashed for their humps.
We hid, like outlaws, those who lived,
in what forests were left.

Yes, squirrel, you have an answer
for this morning's news,
the sight of us?
That one, perhaps two, might have survived,
if eyes do not deceive,
might love indeed,
someday as common as grass?

Question from squirrel: did you say *love?*

No, I said, *live.*
Live someday as common as grass.

All due respect, you said, *love,*
anyone reading this poem can see that plain.

That isn't even grammatical, your mind is squirreling.
And I wouldn't say love *is common,*
even if you *could* say "love common as grass."
It is as rare as a rare red fox, sighted in alpine heights.
(Ah, indeed, live, love:
loved fox one day be *common as grass?*)

I wonder, Professor Fox, says squirrel,
no, this is me asking,
squirrel could not conceive such question,
to what you attribute this joy in your leaping presence
once again in our world?
Our hearts leaping Wordsworths to behold a rainbow in the sky?

Says fox, not that I think it is deserved good news, totally, that we may yet live;
not that you deserve the glory of the sight of our fur,
a red cloud,
orange current rushing in the grass, always a blur,
but the trees can say.
The trees stand for us, rooted and flying,
live, *love*, trees think it's simple, the same thing,
what can't be without the other, says Professor Fox.
If you need me, if you grieve me, listen to earth, singing about me in trees.

I've always lived in poetry, adds the fox,
I'm Hughes thought-fox, I'm Rich's dream,
Clifton's "dear," tutor of The Little Prince,
sleep of Merwin,
I'm in Khartoum in 2006 with Al-Saddig Al-Raddi,
even the moralists,
Aesopian, citing my love of grapes,
like you, Poet, by love of chickens,
like you my wise guy ways (hey hedgehog)—

Wait, you said, says squirrel now, *by love of* chickens,
did you mean, *my* love of chickens?

I said, **my** *love of* . . .

No, you said, **by** *love of* . . . It's here for all to see.

So I step in, the writer of this poem,
on the news I read of scientists sighing,
I mean sighting,
I do mean sighing, too: Sierra rare red fox spied,
who have died, alive again today,
not all dead, giving us now another chance
to let them live, in their crafty ways:
what am I saying, another chance for us, to *love*,
I mean *live*, I mean *love*, I do mean love,
well, *live* perhaps by *love of*,
our crafty leaping love of,
heaping love of,
this world's fox-loved nests, whir and wings:
love, learning earth's wild voice that speaks in trees,
and fox in us,
we who live poetry.

PIGEON / OYSTERS

The pigeon collecting poppies from commemorative field where soldiers died. To build a nest.

Once pigeons delivered messages on the battlefield.
They dared fly for us,
humans who could not understand each other,
or agree to get along.

I consider nature in our lives, of our lives.

The octopus who loves us and possibly is lonely,
who has an octave of love notes for us
and ways to stroke our limbs.

Oysters and why we consider them excellent
for health and celebration.
Why we say the world is my oyster.

There are so many things to say
about how to love a world.

The looks of it are rugged, rough, definitely jagged,
Ridges in ruffles, waves,
pointy peaks of geological delicacy, breech.
Woodlike lines like a bark tree ring, arcs.
Its edges are shoreline, kelpy beach.

Some have barnacles,
hilltop villages of little hollow volcanic cones,
homes where many, many creatures have lived, cooked, loved,
swept by the currents of fate,
the tides of mighty doomed defiance and loss.

They are multicolored, colors of dawn and beach,
sand and kelp,
moss and olive branch, bone and charcoal.

They are formless, each unique,
an irregular shape of foot,
holding unseen a messy, blobby, slimy, slippery life,
in throbbing ethos,
a shimmering iridescence, an unearthly smoothness
the texture of ice, stone,
the color of starlight, a white moon.

To say, the world is my oyster,
outside the Urgent Care on Thirteenth Street,
where forty years ago I was here with child,
then in my belly.
I was the oyster, my womb impenetrable perfection, my baby this pulsing life,
and for all practical purposes ready to come through this wave, tasting brine,
tasting fresh rush of moon's tide,
overtaking one's balance and poise.

This life safe inside me, for now, until I'm opened,
and then the world's, gulped.

I swallow whole this world, its brine, its salt,
its fresh freshness,
and inside I'm clean and new.

I give birth to what will struggle and die,
but not before we learn to see our fate
as shelled beauty—
pried open it is beauty and beauty, and beauty,
such beauty.

COHO

COHO
When Edible Is a Happy Ending for All

Coho, it isn't just you.
It's me, too.
Once you are strength moving through water,
silver flow,
gleaming in sunshine, shining scales, on your way.
And now, you're bagged,
I'm eating you,
my afternoon treat.
And while I think of your life,
how it ended this way,
I realize that someday
that's me, too,
not eaten perhaps in just this way—
but wouldn't that be nice,
if I were so nutritious,
of such worth,
if eating me would make some creature
lustrous and glow,
if I were good to its health?
Though perhaps in whatever form
I become as part of earth
I will feed the waving trees
and worm who is feast to some bird,
and when we think of what the river would need
it would be nice to think in such poem
this prayer is heard.

But God Be With The Clown

MOUSE

The Ridiculous Cheerfulness of a Mouse
—" that idiot optimist mouse . . relentlessly cheerful"
Mickey Mouse in the words of the British press

Cheerfulness is my weapon
I brandish like Cyrano's sword.

When I was five I was mentioning going on tv
The Mickey Mouse Club.
I may have said,
When I am on The Mickey Mouse Club,
something like that.

Barbara, my mother said,
you can't dance, you can't sing,
you have no talent,
you will never be a Mouseketeer.

This may sound harsh now,
and at the time, I was stunned,
my future suddenly opening up in ways
I had not up to that point imagined.
It had seemed pretty defined, my future,
being part of the Mouseketeers.
I only realize now how the concept of Mouseketeers was a play on *musketeers*,
the camaraderie and bonhomie of pirates,
another kind of stage for cahoots.

What, then, would I be? I did not know.

At some point, I became a professor,
lecturing in many countries
on the meaning of Mickey Mouse,
who is remarkable for his resilience.
It does not matter what happens to him,
one of the runts of the animal kingdom,
neither the largest nor the most intelligent

nor the most dangerous,
nor the most beautiful, or mysterious;
as a creature in folklore he is worth a scream or two,
a leap to a chair, a rolling pin, sometimes a fainting, although this is rare.
But whatever happens to the Mouse,
he springs right back,
ever cheerful and bright and determined.

It is odd that the British would denigrate him
as an idiot—
or at least one British journalist
scorns this cartoon character,
when the Mouse seems above all to me
a Winston Churchill
who will never, never, never, never, never give up.
Yes, this mouse was hero and role model,
foe to spirit pierced by its dagger's gleam,
foe at slump, at the dance of brightness.

My mother later told me,
I did not want you to be disappointed.
I did not want you to be hurt.

She knew the world.
She loved me more.

I think now of what I would say to my children,
what I have said when they were five:
you are too big to be a gymnast (I believe she was).

But the Mouse spirit who never gives up
is not concerned.
What any mouse could tell you,
is that dancing and singing and gymnastery
are special talents of mice,
and they have a club that anyone can join,
where you scamper optimistically,
and never notice fear or worry

that shuts down our understanding of where we can go.

Everywhere in the world I spoke,
people loved the Mouse,
and the only way I could explain his character
was to sing and dance,
and no one noticed that I had no talent.

Of course you had talent, my mother said,
I just thought of you in a different kind of life,
and the truth is, I love this life.
I am on stage, on the page, singing and dancing,
I can no longer lecture standing up,
but oh, I am dancing!

Maybe, you *could* be a gymnast, I tell my daughter now.

She is surprised.
Oh, I love doing gymnastics!

You do? I thought I had discouraged you.
She says, Mommy, I knew you were joking.
Of course you would not discourage me!

So you see, optimism is always proven right.

DRAGONFLY

How I'm Taught Green

It is only a reed—nothing to see,
this single green stalk growing
like a flagpole without flag.
It could be a weed, wild,
how it grows by the river, free,
unplanted by any hand—
a dart of random green.
Then the dragonfly visits, sits, straddles it.
This translucent gauze, lace with eyes,
and now I see the stalk with wonder
and in my surprise at how precious,
no, beyond value, how much it means to the fly,
this moment of green in its life—
no, the simple green stroke, dash,
with knuckles like some finger,
simple and so singular,
to this winged creature is the world.

And to me, now, not the stalk of green,
pencil-thin, with which I could write—
not the winged amazement of intricacy,
you can see through the color, the lace,
it's the togetherness of it, the cling,
how now it's a flagpole with a flag,
and flower with its bloom,
a finished entity, complete, a radiance, such grace—
I stand and marvel,
how the dragonfly teaches me what's here,
what matters, what's still, what flutters,
my heart now a bloom, at this sight—
how I'm taught, what's good if you're designed to fly,
this humble moment of green needing you,
needing your visit to be seen for what it is,
a glorious thing,
and you needing its plain being:
one home in mud, one home in air,
this is where the meteor lands—
what I want to say is I'm seeing love
as how the universe works—
dragonfly's kiss, need's patience,
a happiness, one embrace.

GLACIER

Dining on Glacier

"To dine with a glacier on a sunny day is a glorious thing and makes feasts of meat and wine ridiculous. The glacier eats hills and drinks sunbeams." John Muir

The white mountain outside the window is the elephant in the room, the lodge
dining room,
or perhaps it is the bear.
I call to mind how John Muir felt it was glorious—
his word he added to everything
like some people salt their food—
to dine with a glacier.

On my plate is smoked salmon,
tasting of river flesh and fire, of iridescent flies,
of sweeping current.
On my plate are blueberries, and I tongue sky,
as Muir "far and high in the mountains" with bread gone takes in manzanita
berries "like a bear."
Yes, I can taste the sap as I behold
the trees at the base of the peak,
I can taste what hummingbirds sip and eagles,
far higher up, find, in my eggs,
and my potatoes, buttered with sun.
The nuts on my plate, tasting of trailhead,
with notes of moss,
and I realize I am eating the diet of a bear,
a good look on bears,
not so much on me, who waddles as it is.
Emerson exhorted us to be abstemious,
favoring air and dew,
thus Emily Dickinson's "inebriate of air am I,
and debauchee of dew."
This was Muir's diet,
which he saw in his fellow journey companion,
the being of a glacier, whom he joined eating hills
and drinking sunbeams, with relish and gusto.

They say the most he weighed was 148
and one time returned from a trip at 90.
He ate "God's abounding, inexhaustible spiritual beauty bread."
This explains his answer to what kind of bread he took to the mountains: "just bread."

But I taste this biscuit before me, with strawberry jam,
and I know I am eating the soil itself,
its seeds, the wind, the rain and ice,
the whoosh of storm, the foam of cloud, which I spoon.
I am not dining with a glacier, I am dining on glacier,
and my insides are chilled and thrilled.
I look around the room at my fellow diners,
who are quiet.
How can this be,
when we are eating such news of creation?
I remember the story,
that when John Muir was recovering from an illness,
he went on a hike, promising not to exert himself.
He found himself on top of a mountain, leaping for joy, "the glory, the glory!"
His companions shook their heads at him.
What is wrong with *you*, he shouted.
How can you stand there reserved?

Not me.
I would leap, if I could,
leap up and exclaim at such feast.
How is everyone so calm, eating earth?
I sip my ice water, and sing,
a song of wind in me,
river, sweetness, sap, majesty.

DEER

You Have Seen This Scene in Sixty Paintings, Except the Tangerine and the Deer

Not only does the deer have no idea
about private property,
which makes sense; it is young.
But it is not in the least shaken when I appear naked,
nor when I exclaim, Shoo, Scram!
And wave my alabaster and hanging arms.
Maybe it does not know what those words mean, yet,
and I try,
Away!

I suppose it thinks it is only natural
for another creature to be its strange self in the garden.
My swaying breasts and bobbing belly
are not intimidating.
If my nakedness was intended to startle,
it is I who is startled to find myself so,
by the sight of a deer
eating my sunflowers and canna lilies.

Aroused? I am crazed.
Certainly my own heart is racing
as I charge outside holding a towel,
having espied a deer through the window
as I emerge from the bath.
Who knew I could move so fast?
My husband's garden in which he labors every day,
beset by deer coming to eat (and often kill)
the young trees and plants,
which have tasty tender sprouts—
I am every gardener's avenging angel.
I am leaping and shouting,
a language meant to change some creature's mind,
but the deer stands still.
It has looked up from eating.

Impassive and wondering, it regards me.
Words, leaps, nakedness, I've pulled out all I've got.
None of it matters—
my words, leaps, nakedness
belong in this garden,
just like the deer, munching away;
I am just part of the garden
like the trees in the wind,
the jay in the aspen.

Only my husband's hearing my shouts
(alternating between Go! Scram! And, CHRISter!)
and running to hurl a tangerine in its direction
moves the deer to dash about towards the fence,
and finally,
to bound away.

(Well, it will say when it gets home,
I had an interesting experience today.)

My husband surveys me now,
naked and barefoot on the stones.
It has come to this.

He spends seven hours a day on this garden
designed to be "low maintenance,"
working along with the Creator on behalf of earth,
in this little plot of land we call ours, but fence in vain.

We both know we can never keep the deer out.
To own a garden, ha ha,
is to realize all we do not own,
cannot own,
never have owned,
and to be returned to our senses—
our natural states in which we are mythic,
heroic,
humbled in realizing
on which side the bread is buttered.

KOI

The Koi Loves Me Back

In the pond by Houston's in Pasadena,
there live orange and white koi a foot long
and wide as your spread-out fingers,
and they are ornamental,
like bulbs on a Christmas tree, or earrings.

But as I looked at them in wonder,
their colors, their choreography,
they swam up to me mouths open wide
in astonishment and awe.

They were gaping at me.
I was no one, a nameless, anonymous ephemera.
What were they seeing?
Their mouths moved.
What were they saying?

I remember my mother in her last days with me,
opening her mouth and earnestly talking to me,
but I could not make out the words,
only the insides of words.

I just could see her eyes,
putting all she wanted to say into her eyes,
looking at me.

Koi, are you bringing me news of my mother
who cannot be heard, but can be understood,
as we watch the beauty of you,
your shining, your glistening, your splash?

The beauty of someone telling you they see you.
That is what she said to me,
what I figure out she said.

I hear it now.

She says, You're here.
I see you.

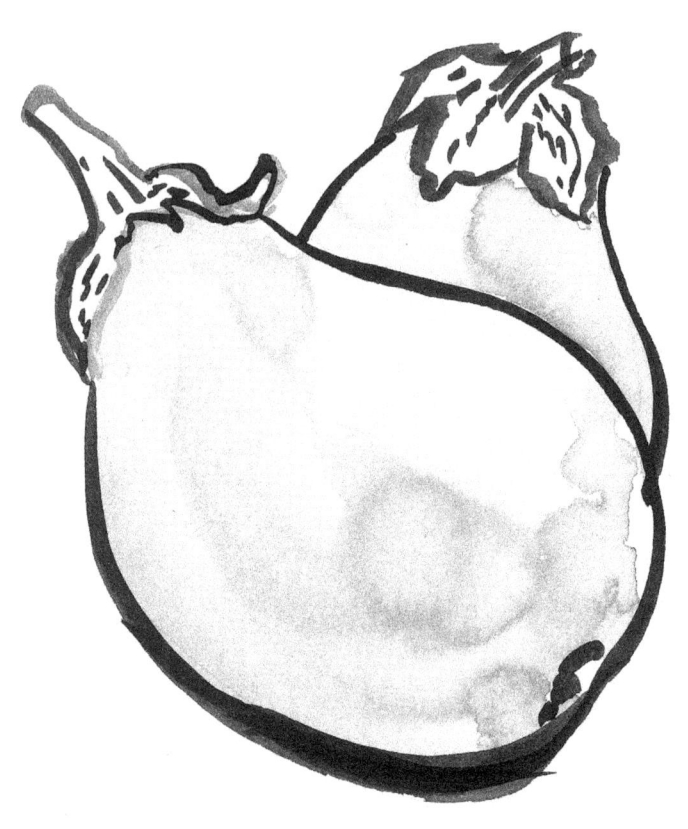

EGGPLANT

Milanese Turns Out to Be Gateway Grief

Don't be afraid to read this.
Yes, I said grief. It happens. It is happening to me.

For example, this morning, in a crossword puzzle clue,
What is dipped in egg, then breadcrumbs, then fried in oil?

Now you would think I would know this,
because this is in fact what I do with eggplants
and also tomatoes
that my son,
who consorts with chefs, and is one,
taught me.

He didn't approve of eggplants personally
but as long as I was going to make them,
he showed me a method.

I loved it—
how it made the vegetable a crispy sandwich
of a tender hot squish,
a dissolution of something hard,
broken down into an absolute lightness.

But I could not, could not, come up with the word,
even though I had "I" as the second letter
(for pilfer, Down).
I finally broke down and looked it up,
because it was the key to everything else around it.
Milanese!

So that is what they call what I was doing—
I've ordered it;
I just never thought of how it came about.
So my son had made me
without my realizing it
into a kind of chef-lite.

I was thinking I would call him,
even though it is too early,
he would still be sleeping
after some all-nighter of projects and pacing,
and I would say, tell me about Milanese.

And he would put down the clippers or soldering iron
or any tool I had no name for,
and go into a cultural history
of the practice
and the difference
between Milan and Naples
and Bologna and Rome,
and who knows what he would tell me.

It would be a lot.
I wouldn't have time for it
but I would be fascinated.

I would get some wine
and sit down and put him on speaker
and just savor what he was saying,
what he knew,
his world knowledge that had happened
totally without me.

We would agree to make Milanese
the next time we are together.

And with this thought,
I am struck, my heart is struck as if with a bat,
no, not like that;
yes, the pain,
but it is a swell of sorrow,
I am filled with silent tears,
and shock,
that he is not here to call;
he is gone.

Oh, I am thinking of so many poets right now,
Gerald Manley Hopkins,
in despair over his aspens dear,
all felled, felled, felled!

Embarrassingly, it is like that.
It really is.
How could you strand me, I think,
going forward with my life,
with a knowledge of Milanese?

Who knows what else you taught me
that I do not have words for,
that I know and have yet to learn.

So I come to you, my Reader,
who don't know anything about this,
and I'm firm,
even shining lustrously on the outside—
I've been battered, and fried,
and I'm tender on the inside,
a squishy mess,
but light.

And you also have been through this,
and now I am telling you the word for it,
so you can figure out the puzzle too.

CAT

Animals That Saw You: Garbo

The worst cat—no one, even her owner, disputes that.
She creeps up our apple tree to gain access to our deck
and leap upon our unsuspecting guests,
seated at the table
(much shrieking and crockery cracking clatter).
She lies belly up in front of our door,
in wait like the spider in the web, to be petted,
then attack—she scratched everybody.

We buy the advertised fancy mattress
for our renovated bedroom
and she sneaks in the house
and pees on it the first night—
Christer and I secretly think
the other is excreting and oozing.

We end up having to have the brand-new mattress cleaned.

She leaps on my shoulder
when I'm getting out of the car in my driveway,
or in my lap when I'm seated reading in the front yard
—I'm allergic but dare not move.

She sleeps unwelcome on our welcome mat—
yet when she died we cried.
It wasn't that she wanted to get us.
It was that she got us—and didn't care.

So what is it she saw in us,
we who shrank and kept our distance,
respecting the scratch
(and of course the dander which she couldn't help)?
She saw our fear, and she poked it.
She saw through it, through to our helpless love, which she knew was there—
she never doubted.

She forgave us our fear, rubbing up against us, purring, relaxed on our doorstep,
pouncing on us, leaping on us, engaging with us,
at every chance she got.

And—we liked it;
we liked her there
—secretly—each of us.
This was amazing to us and we could not explain it.
But of course
it is the most explainable thing I have ever written.

WHO PONDERS THIS TREMENDOUS SCENE

BEE

"Does This Pollen Make My Butt Look Big?"
Asks Illustrator Christine Crozier

The squirrel does not worry, could someone love me?
The dragonfly does not fret,
am I having a good wing day?
The birch does not say am I growing bald?
The grass, the worm, the willow, the rose, the bear,
do not say, I will not feed today; I want to look good for my mate (in some cases
my other end).
The mountain does not despair
of losing itself with each rain,
nor rock exclaim its pebble fate—
nor pebble its own sand future.
They do not doubt their beauty.
Can they know their magnificence?

Glam bee, you tell me, if you know you are amazing?
All your parts, your fashion sense,
how your flight is dance,
how many eyes you have to see color?
You do not worry, nor do you know all you know.

But such delicacy, such complexity, such color,
your design—
perhaps our human brain is meant to see our world with wonder,
to see tremendousness,
to have a vocabulary for scale in which to be awed.
Perhaps our brains are meant
to ponder our Fellow Mortals,
As our own beauty,
which would have us eaten, stung, sung.

TURKEY

I mean God! to have a turkey in your day

Well, I don't know how you would get anywhere.

You would be on your way, your keys out.
Your ironed shirt, your books, your charged phone.
Your plans, your scheduled first meeting,
your appointment, your first customer—
you're busy. You're on your way.
You're barely on time.
But you can make it.
Your mind is elsewhere.
What he said.
What she meant. What could happen.

Then.
A movement to the side of your car,
or maybe off the bike path.
And there.

Its span is enormous!
It's as big as a cooler across—or planet rover—
but jerking.
A feathered caramel strutting,
sleek neck arched, swiveling,
chin raised in a hauteur mien.

It's all business, this flurry of feathers
and upwards tail spread out in fanlike majesty.
It's a surrey with the fringe on top.

You—well not you, but people,
possibly think of a turkey
as a neatly folded centerpiece,
folded into itself on the table,
an organized oval
on the Norman Rockwell magazine cover.
But this before you is a construction by an artist

who deals with large-scale objects,
an installation, a Flash Mob prank—
a surprisingly endearing face
with large dark eyes against a bald whiteness,
like an owl,
and then this red tie hanging down,
a bib the texture of a thick Navaho blanket,
a cravat really.
Its body is swirls and circles,
almost a full circle of a tail,
as if you or I were carrying across our backs
a small windmill filled in with ruffled canvas,
a structure heavy as a pitchfork or boat anchor—
if it were lighter it would sail.

Maybe it does sail.

Maybe it will take off in a wind,
like a kite.
The turkey is a kind of feathered boat,
some craft harboring in our neighborhood street,
or in the parking lot in front of the courthouse,
giving the city a farmish feel,
a humanness.
How is it that a creation on stilts,
strutting twigs,
suddenly rises up to a tree,
a tree we didn't even notice,
and how does the pencil limb hold such an engine,
such a weighted being,
freighted with tassels and Inca headdress?

How can you get your mind
around a feathered flag flying colors frankly out there,
bold, geometric, indigenous—
you see this palate in earliest native art.

Sometimes the bald head is summer sky blue,
and the neck cravat and shawl
are pink and yellow and orange,
a rainbow trout look,
such peculiar grandeur.

We call people who are characters *turkeys*?
Urban slang for ongoing screw ups, "
a loser, a dud, naïve, inept, stupid, a failure"—
because we don't know,
perhaps we never have known,
how to comprehend such a phenomenon,
a circus of architectural features happening
all at once.

You can't put it all together—it's too complex to see.
You're lost in the mismatch,
skinny poles holding up Queen Victoria and her carriage,
haughty and not scared.
Neither of them.

Oh, what if Benjamin Franklin's idea prevailed,
and the turkey were our national image?

Perhaps it is best it is not,
as you don't want to see your symbol
served up with mashed potatoes and cranberry sauce,
and dividing eaters into dark meat and white meat.

And turkeys are too improbable for pavement,
too theatrical for sidewalks,
for ways we have organized
and perhaps lost ourselves.

But now here's a chance—here's a chance.
Let's talk turkey.

Because you don't see
how you can just go on with your day now.
How can you?

This is not a 911,
this is not a case of animal protection service,
but this might be a call to the office,
a sick day much deserved,
a special holy day observed.
You can turn around,
and consider your life.

You are on your path, now,
because in all your dizziness of business,
you came upon turkey's splendor of busyness,
stopping traffic in your tracks,
your own amazement running amuck.

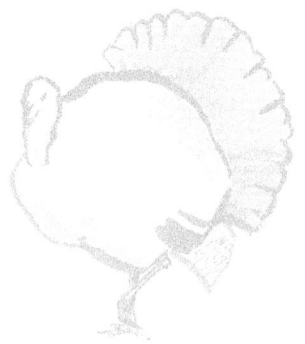 

TURNIP

There Comes a Time for Happiness

Happiness waits its turn,
like the turnips you bought
(because the purple)
and the parsnips
(your father fried them in butter—
no one had ever heard of them,
and this was a sign of his weirdness
but now you bought them
because you miss him
and they turn out to be delicious)
you put on the shelf and forgot.

One morning before the sun rose,
but you knew it was going to be a glorious day,
clear, bright, leaves still on some trees,
yellow and orange and brown,
and big ones floating to earth,
air-skiing, they called it among themselves,
and sometimes,
if you are so lucky,
landing on you,
it's their choice,
your holding out your arms
and even running does no good,
they come to you on their own volition,
you were in your plaid bathrobe,
and you had writing to do, papers to grade,
so of course you were at the stove,
wondering what you should cook.

Your eyes fell upon the forgotten turnips, and parsnips,
so withered you almost might have thrown them out,
someone else would have thrown them out.

But oh Lord they were amazing.

They were now beyond vegetable
(that ship had sailed).
They transcended vegetable.

The turnips had grown whiskers on one end,
white scraggly whiskers,
almost cobwebby, and on the other end,
had grown some kind of purple green sea flower
like an urchin in a tidepool lit by morning light,
rufflesy,
surrounded by bright green moss.
The parsnips resembled your own skin,
your thigh in this decade of wrinkles, withering.

They were so beautiful you stood there and beheld,
and you knew you were seeing glory,
the way that earth (a short-timer)
and sun (also a short-timer but in a larger way)
orbits, rotates, and spins,
and the world turns orange and red and crimson
and cochineal and scarlet and purple and gold,
and you rejoice in these changes,
this movement that moves you,
gladdens you,
peacens you,
and you realize
you are looking at the beauty of yourself
in these roots that have taken on a new life,
out of ground, sprouting flowers and shoots.

And you begin to cut these up,
the firm white perfect flesh,
and put in water and salt
and cut up a lemon
(first squeezing it on your hand
to erase your speckled brown spots)

and add a sprig of rosemary from your front yard
(you're barefoot in the freezing morning
as you cut it and inhale the fragrance in the darkness, the plant's hello and kiss).

And in the red pot, over fire,
water, roots, glisten, and shine,
this message of earth, of what it means
to live now on this planet,
becoming, becoming,
and who knows what I'm sprouting as I wither,
who knows who will find me
pure inside, intact,
and beautiful.

Who knows to whom or what I can be so nutritious,
so delicious.
Who knows when happiness will appear,
and who knew it lives in what is forgotten,
depleted, whiskered,
what you have in you yet to make what,
it turns out,
stirring, tasting,
is amazing.

GOLDFISH

The Improbability of Orange

You might ask me why I drive south
four hundred miles
to feed the fish.
You already think you know
and like to hear that it is because
since my father's death
I am trying to maintain his pond,
the one he built with his own hands
out of stones he collected and carried his whole life,
the one he had blueprints for
when he went into the hospital
and emerged, I believed, to get this job done.

Done, he made a wooden sign (now faded),
I Have Made This,
set next to the pond,
and what I know about filters and waterfall hydraulics and algae and Ph
would fit into this line.
I couldn't even open the fish food container,
which was stuck,
and even when I did
and scattered flakes on the surface,
there were no fish to be seen.
The pond's water, so dark and murky.

Perhaps they had died.

And then it was cold, perhaps freezing in the night.
And the raccoons.
And the heron.
And the neighbor cat.
And the water evaporated in the afternoons.
And then it overflowed, and a fish was floating.

Now on my To Do list was *pet store*.
Green fish in a bag.
These aren't the right ones, I said.

They are supposed to be orange.
When they grow, the boy who helped me said.
They will have to establish the pond, he said.
Whatever that meant!

I would litter the surface with flakes, no fish in sight,
and still I drove,
and went out barefoot every morning,
worried what I would find.
Between the night's wild dangers
and all I did not know—
still stood and scattered flakes looking for signs of—
and there they were,
stripes of orange in the dark, green, water,
the fish,
who had survived the night,
the frost, the quick paws.

These darting moments of orange,
arcs of orange,
how did they become,
how did they survive?

Today I wake up and still undressed
I hurry outside to behold a miracle,
orange against dark and green.

The pond is established,
and this mystery makes the dark water,
the green water,
what I love—so improbable,
the orange makes me love such a world,
what can live in it.

This is what I feed, this dark world,
in all my incompetence,
which doesn't matter after all,
this is what I care for.

LOON

Why

You can hammer crooked nails,
catch the grandfather bass.

You can make me laugh.

You could persuade a moose
to tickle you in the morning.

When you are wrong, I am nervous,
clouds drown.
I'd rather have the earth wrinkle.

You can make up a song and sing it so I'm lazy.
Your calloused hands feel good.

When your face gets red you taste good.
You could make a pine tree sorry it littered needles.

It seems safe to go to sleep when you are there.

When you are gone
the moon is sharp-edged, and the wind chokes.

You can finesse the bones out of the pickerel.

You can hammer crooked nails,
catch the grandfather bass,
you can make me laugh,
when I know we will die,
you can make me glad
like the loon
with the bass in her belly.

RIVER

When I Die You Don't Have to Divert the River for Me

Fragments of an epic text found in Me-Turan (modern Tell Haddad) relate that at the end of his life Gilgamesh was buried under the river bed. The people of Uruk diverted the flow of the Euphrates passing Uruk for the purpose of burying the dead king within the river bed.

But it would be nice.

The river I am thinking of is the Merced, of course,
River of Mercy,
flowing as if the vanity of earth,
which loves rivers,
is redeemed here—
The rocks tell you everything—
John Muir says they sing, they preach—
this river by the Chapel
I have lain beside
on the gleaming gold-stuff in the sand,
and leaped into,
or rather, hopped,
on an afternoon in Yosemite,
and my father's ashes in this stream,
and my mother's—
and to get me underneath this river,
so that it flows over me,
you would have to enlist the moon to move closer,
you could do that,
it loves music,
you could get someone to play the cello,
and a flute,
and it would come close,
as it does when it thinks no one is watching—
and the water would leap up like a trout,
arc for the fly moon,
and in that moment,
you would have picnic hampers

for the people who have come to watch
and say, cheerfully, "I love hard work,
I could watch it for hours,"
and they would be eating
Julia Child's train sandwiches,
loaves with unsweetened butter and ham
that have been sat on for the journey,
and are now warm and squashed,
with gherkins,
and raspberries smelling of soap,
and some whiskey,
the river would arc over the picnickers
in a stream like a rainbow,
and now you would get your team with shovels
to quickly dig into the fools' gold river bottom ,
and make a little dent for my bones.

Meanwhile the river is now
on the other side of the meadow,
but as I said,
you don't have to divert the river.
It will spring back of its own accord,
and will rush over my spirit
alive again today
in the trout's freckles and the rock's speckles
and star matter.

WHALE

This Thing We Call Friendship
Is Bigger Than We Know

Luna the whale aka L98 or Tsuux'iit, wanted only to be our friend. Every day, the Canadian Department of Fisheries and Oceans said, she got into trouble: the more she tried to engage us, the more she was an outlaw. Humans—Mowachaht/Muchalaht First Nation, journalists, teachers, tourists—were written up. Cited. Booked. Their crime—and they did get fined: it was looking the whale in the eye. Looking was proscribed. By law, no one could relate to the whale. Ignore it—the official policy.

And yet the whale did not understand. It swam up to the boats, grabbed a hose with its mouth, and sprayed the folks on deck. It made all its entreating sounds. Don't look at it, people were told. Look away. You are robbing it of its whaleness. It never can become a real whale and go back to a pod life if you allow it to experience humans as its community.

But some came to believe that ignoring the whale was cruel. They felt criminally implicated. One man finally decided—he was a writer—Luna (it turned out he was a he) wants friendship. It was like Huckleberry Finn: *I'll go to hell! I will look him in the eye. Come what may.*

I'm not going to say here that the government backed off, in the face of citizen insurrection, civic insurgency, and that it was a happy ending. Well, it was a happy ending, but it is not one that saved the whale's life. They wanted to imprison the whale, cage it as a danger. The First Nation, eldercare, the elementary school, used song and dance to encourage the whale to resist capture. It was a tug of war, engines vs. boats paddled by grade-school singers, secretaries, wrinkled matriarchs, it was government vs. the people. It was we the people as at first, at last.

A journalist who came for three weeks to report on the goings on stayed three years, called to friendship. He said, "This thing we call friendship is bigger than we know." A whale who wanted to be a friend broke down the boundaries of who we are as people, extending enfranchisement to species with a big heart.

Certainly Luna was the biggest hearted friend he had.

It turns out we learn about friendship from a slippery and leaping creature, and that the possibilities for friendship are infinite in this universe. Luna was killed by a tugboat's propeller—the fishermen they said hated the whale and wanted it dead—but here we see, none of us who watched the news reports wanted this whale dead.

We all felt we were its friend. We all cried to lose him. Our lives were changed. He was the friendship teacher. Oh, yes, this is the happy ending. We learned about friendship, something bigger than we know.

This Thing We Call Friendship Is Bigger Than We Know

Luna the whale aka L98 or Tsuux'iit, wanted only to be our friend. Every day, the Canadian Department of Fisheries and Oceans said, she got into trouble: the more she tried to engage us, the more she was an outlaw. Humans—Mowachaht/Muchalaht First Nation, journalists, teachers, tourists—were written up. Cited. Booked. Their crime—and they did get fined: it was looking the whale in the eye. Looking was proscribed. By law, no one could relate to the whale. Ignore it—the official policy.

And yet the whale did not understand. It swam up to the boats, grabbed a hose with its mouth, and sprayed the folks on deck. It made all its entreating sounds. Don't look at it, people were told. Look away. You are robbing it of its whale-ness. It never can become a real whale and go back to a pod life if you allow it to experience humans as its community.

But some came to believe that ignoring the whale was cruel. They felt criminally implicated. One man finally decided—he was a writer—Luna (it turned out he was a he) wants friendship. It was like Huckleberry Finn: *I'll go to hell! I will look him in the eye. Come what may.*

I'm not going to say here that the government backed off, in the face of citizen insurrection, civic insurgency, and that it was a happy ending. Well, it was a happy ending, but it is not one that saved the whale's life. They wanted to imprison the whale, cage it as a danger. The First Nation, eldercare, the elementary school, used song and dance to encourage the whale to resist capture. It was a tug of war, engines vs. boats paddled by grade-school singers, secretaries, wrinkled matriarchs, it was government vs. the people. It was we the people as at first, at last.

A journalist who came for three weeks to report on the goings on stayed three years, called to friendship. He said, "This thing we call friendship is bigger than we know." A whale who wanted to be a friend broke down the boundaries of who we are as people, extending enfranchisement to species with a big heart.

Certainly Luna was the biggest hearted friend he had.

It turns out we learn about friendship from a slippery and leaping creature, and that the possibilities for friendship are infinite in this universe. Luna was killed by a tugboat's propeller—the fishermen they said hated the whale and wanted it dead—but here we see, none of us who watched the news reports wanted this whale dead.

We all felt we were its friend. We all cried to lose him. Our lives were changed. He was the friendship teacher. Oh, yes, this is the happy ending. We learned about friendship, something bigger than we know.

OCTOPUS

How I Became a Vegetarian

It wasn't even watching *My Octopus Teacher*,
although that made me cry,
and know that I would never again eat calamari,
which I love, with lemon,
and perhaps I would want to adopt an octopus
for my living room,
but could I be so loved, so loved?
So forgiven?
You would have to rise to the occasion,
and be worthy of such love.

Entreated, petted with eight reaching out arms:
can you bear to be its Person?
Its The One?

Okay, yes, I love you, too.
My husband will understand.

Maybe.

All this I was thinking as I was weeping,
standing at the glass at The Monterey Aquarium.
She was the shape of the corner of the tank,
crouched and huddled,
and changed shape and color as I stood there,
staring.
A face.

People were suddenly in my peripheral vision.
They were giving me space.
Time disappeared.

Coats next to me—
We spoke inner language to each other,
goodbye for now.
My heart is expanded.

I move over,
left to the tank of its sister creature,
the squid.

Have I ever seen a squid,
besides in pieces on a plate?

And this squid swam right to the glass in front of me,
Sideways staring,
and there the two of us were,
eye to eye,
locked in an embrace of vision.

Neither of us moved.
Our eyes held fast.
We were in some spaceship transfer,
and exchanged our souls.

Finally, we had the same soul.

Oh, I was crying?

Perhaps it was not crying,
this having tears run down my face.

Perhaps it was to be as wet and silent
and staring and close.

I had never had such an experience
of seeing eye to eye.

Our bodies fell away;
skin, scales,
they did not matter.
They were no matter.
We existed in the same plane.

Neither of us moved.

Minutes, minutes.
This enormous eye locked on mine,
holding fast, beholding.

We were fastened.

Finally my daughter,
another creature to whom I am fastened,
put her arm around me,
to comfort me—she knew—
it was not grief, or maybe it was,
and it was only this one arm around me that enabled me to leave,
this human love,
and I wondered,
I wonder now,
how we could love each other like this?

With ten arms —ten arms, hooks and suckers,
and the largest eye,
I could say, the squid in me, the octopus of me,
holds you tight.
You are loved by an army.
The squid of me sees you.
Sees you.

RIVER

You Are Not Not Moving
in a Happening Illimitably World

You see me not moving at all,
on this bench,
but so much is happening.
Hearing the river,
brain's wind carrying me sound waves
in interior reeds.
Wind's brain at galactic speeds.
The river.

What heap of noise.
Its sounds of swish, layered splash,
a running, a pouring,
The river moving by gravity.
Feeling sun's waves.
Its warmth on my forehead.

My heart pumping.
Blood pulsing in my veins and arteries.
Breath in and out,
wind filling its tree branches like lungs.
Inhaling fragrance of cedar.
In-hailing.

Seeing light on water.
Trees growing down and up and out.
Leaves turning colors. Leaves falling.
Stones disintegrating. Sand forming.
Sun warming leg and foot and neck
and hand on right side.
Clouds moving.
Earth turning. Earth spinning.
Sun revolving. Galaxy revolving.
White water bounces.
Water shines and glistens.
A shadow grows on the ground

by the rock across the pebbles.
Unseen fish hold to the current.
My mind's eyes and ears and nostrils and skin awake.

I can hardly fathom all this happening—
Noisy rambunctious restless racing swirling upside down floating carrying on.

Sitting on this bench
Not moving at all.

THIS WHOLE EXPERIMENT OF GREEN

PIGEON

Casserole: A Natural History

Sartre was outraged on behalf of the Party by such episodes as the "affair of the carrier pigeons," in which the Party Secretary was found with pigeons in his car and was accused by the police of using them, like a good revolutionary, to coördinate illegal demonstrations. (It turned out that, like a good Frenchman, he was merely planning a squab casserole.)—Adam Gopnik, "Facing History," *New Yorker*, 12 April 2012

Once upon a time, foxes, sly villains of childen's literature, were our pets, intelligent and loyal, until they figured out how to get at the chickens in the pens, because they shared with us a love of chickens. They became outlaws and hat flourishes and coat trim. At least they were not eaten.

I can't imagine a worse fate than being tasty, although when you come to think of it, isn't the history of species on earth (and possibly entities in space—think of the very hungry black holes) the conception of others as tasty?

When I think of the sorrows of my life, all my faults that put me in physical and spiritual peril, all the things I rue, everything ruining and dangerous about me, the things I regret, when I feel most sorry for myself (as my father said, the one true human emotion, self-pity), I say, at least I am not tasty.

Of course that is not true—I am tasty, for example, to the pregnant mosquito who craves my blood for her young, a good cause, I always think, and don't mind contributing, although praying not to get malaria, which did happen to one of my students who died from it. Yes, right in our Vermont dorm, in our day and age. I was trying to tell people this was possible. No one believed it. I was college president at the time, and I could not get over it. You can't.

On the topic of what you can't. In London I was told this story. A man visits a farm and notices a pig with three legs. Why does that pig have three legs? Oh, that pig, the owner says, that pig is remarkable! That pig saved our family from a fire! He came into the house and roused us all and we could escape. He was a hero! When our daughter was going to drown in the pond, he went in and saved her! No one could believe it! When a burglar was going to rob our barn, he ran him off. Yes, the visitor said, but why does he have three legs? The owner says, a pig like that, you don't eat all at once!

I know! Poor pigs. They are so tasty. To be tasty *and* useful. This seems an unfair fate. A compound tragedy. Like pigeons. Pigeons are in human history for many reasons—including, we read, as carriers of messages. They carried messages on battlefields covered with poppies. When these battle fields became graveyards with stones marked by poppies, the pigeons flew off with the poppies to build their nests from them. I don't know what I love more—the image of pigeons aloft with poppies, flying poppies, like banners planes fly to announce something to the crowds below, some kind of message that poppies bring to us, in their fluttery orange voice, or the idea of a nest of poppies, enveloped in and waking up to their bright swallow of sun, and also—bringing new life to the commemoration of those who died, their living on in the safe home where you raise something that flies.

We see pigeons as characters in sober police reports and political history. I don't know how we figured this message-carrying intelligence of theirs out, or who else we may have tried to employ like this first, for example, trying to coax or coerce any number of footed and soaring creatures to get a message to someone, which is hard enough to do even today, with all the telephone and messaging and iPhone and texting and email and UPS and FedEx and one's husband: it still seems daunting and quixotic to imagine something one has to say getting to another being in another place. Telling a bird, go—take this: how do you even get the bird to listen, to stay still, how do you speak pigeon? How does the pigeon recognize your recipient?

You are thinking about owls now in Harry Potter. But isn't that magic?

Clearly I have much to learn.

What do I know about pigeons? Well first of all so little.

I reflect on pigeons in literature. In the historical account of Sartre, we hear a reference to pigeon as tasty to the human tongue. I recall Nathanael Hawthorne's prelude to *The Scarlet Letter*, "The Custom House," which people skip over to get to the story, but I think is really somehow important; it pretends to be true, in a different way than Ken Kesey means when he begins *One Flew Over the Cuckoo Nest*, "this is true even though it did not happen," as good a description of fiction as I have heard. Hawthorne's prologue gives us a man recalling his life, a meal he had half a century earlier containing pigeons in a "decent competency of onion sauce."

There we have it again: pigeons as tasty.

And did not Gertrude Stein reference the sad end of pigeons in the hands of her hungry expatriate compatriot Ernest Hemingway, when she said, "pigeons on the grass, alas," as I imagine she was being slyly literal, knowing of his noonday practice to capture nearby pigeons in the park and take them home to Hadley in a paper bag for lunch.

So, you are saying, is this natural history of the casserole really about pigeons? It seems so. Their being a tasty dish is complicated by our relationship with them as fellow mortals on a common journey, and at the same time, our wiping them out. Did not one of our first American novelists decry the extinction of pigeons? In 1823—we were barely a country—James Fennimore Cooper describes their "slaughter" in *The Pioneers*. Natty Bumpo sets the scene:

> *See, cousin Bess! see, Duke, the pigeon-roosts of the south have broken up! They are growing more thick every instant. Here is a flock that the eye cannot see the end of. There is food enough in it to keep the army of Xerxes for a month and feathers enough to make beds for the whole country. . . . The reports of the firearms became rapid, whole volleys rising from the plain, as flocks of more than ordinary numbers darted over the opening, shadowing the field like a cloud; and then the light smoke of a single piece would issue from among the leafless bushes on the mountain, as death was hurled on the retreat of the affrighted birds, who were rising from a volley, in a vain effort to escape. . .So prodigious was the number of the birds, that the scattering fire of the guns, with the hurtling missiles, and the cries of the boys, had no other effect than to break off small flocks from the immense masses that continued to dart along the valley, as if the whole of the feathered tribe were pouring through that one pass. None pretended to collect the game, which lay scattered over the fields in such profusion as to cover the very ground with the fluttering victims."*

> *The slaughter described finally ended with a grand finale when an old swivel gun was "loaded with handsful of bird-shot," and fired into the mass of pigeons with such fatal effect that there were birds enough killed and wounded on the ground to feed the whole settlement.*

And in "The Chain Bearer" he describes whole skies of pigeons taken down in fluttering chaos.

Speaking of alas, I look up "edible pigeon" on Wikipedia, and Oh.My.God! No! No! This is horrible! There are these entries about how baby pigeons, less than four weeks old, are called "squab," and eaten "hot and moist." And—I did not know this—oh, I don't even want to tell you.

Maybe you knew this, but I did not: under "People Also Ask," there is

> "Pigeons are widely eaten in many countries, including Britain and Ireland. Squab, which is just a young pigeon, is a staple on fancy French restaurant menus. Remember that a pigeon is nothing more than a large dove. So if you love to eat doves – and no hunter I know doesn't – you'll love your pigeons just as much."

Loving doves? As in loving to eat them? Aren't doves the imagery for peace and love?

Wait, wait, wait. I look up the article about this:

> A great many dog trainers work their animals with live pigeons, an unloved bird exempt from game laws in most states. A precious few actually eat their pigeons after the training session, however, a sad state of affairs that ought to change.

> After all, you should remember that Columbia livia, the common rock dove, a/k/a pigeon, was brought to America as food. Pigeons are widely eaten in many countries, including Britain and Ireland. And squab, which is just a young pigeon, is a staple on fancy French restaurant menus. So why don't we eat our pigeons?

> I blame New York City, where legions of pigeons mob old people on park benches, bobbing their little heads for crumbs. City pigeons, wherever they live, eat whatever they can, and can sometimes carry diseases. They give the species a bad rap.

> On the other hand, country pigeons, which are what your training birds are, eat grain, are fat and healthy – and, if you could sell them plucked and pretty to your local fancy restaurant, would fetch a high price.

Remember that a pigeon is nothing more than a large dove. So if you love to eat doves — and no hunter I know doesn't — you'll love your pigeons just as much. It's true, wild barn pigeons can live a long time and get tough, but your training pigeons will be young and tender.

So how to go about it? Pluck your pigeons first. Yes, pluck. Pigeons and doves are ridiculously easy to pluck dry; I can do one in about 60 seconds. Gut and leave your birds whole and roast them, or hell, go ahead and skin a mess of them, fillet off the meat, grind it with pork fat and make the best country pâté you've ever had. Add pigeon meat to sausage. Braise it like duck. Sear the breast meat hot and fast, keeping the center medium-rare like a duck breast and you will have a bite of meat fit for a king.

Looking for ideas? I have a slew of pigeon and dove recipes over on Hunter Angler Gardener Cook. That'll get you started.

Free your mind. Eat your pigeons.

A member of both Pheasants Forever and Quail Forever, Hank Shaw is a hunter, cookbook author and award-winning writer. His website is Hunter Angler Gardener Cook (www.honest-food.net). He lives near Sacramento, CA.

Here are you and I, processing prevailing wind-ideas on how humans—us—dangerously view our world (if you are a pigeon and even if you are not). We hear that the pigeon, aka "common rock dove," is "an unloved bird." It is sort of like when an enthusiastic plant is unwanted in a garden and thus becomes a weed, officially doomed, its ended justified, as not belonging. To be unloved is a fatal fate.

What makes a creature unloved?

What are the perils of being cast out of the community of being?

Ah, but I remember cooing of doves and pigeons. Isn't this our soundtrack of love? I think of Tesla, in his last days holed up in his New York apartment, in love with pigeons. He had what he considered a consensual relationship with a pigeon—reciprocal love. Yes, he did! Listen to this:

> *"Tesla used to take walks to the park to feed the pigeons. He developed an unusual relationship with a white pigeon which used to visit him every day.*
>
> *"I loved that pigeon as a man loves a woman, and she loved me. As long as I had her, there was a purpose to my life," Tesla once said."*

And excuse me, but is it not true that doves are actually not only beloved but considered sacred?

Then, if we keep reading about pigeons, we see illustrations of white doves at the Blue Mosque, then a Table of Contents that includes Paganism, Judaism, Christianity, Islam, Peace and pacifism in politics, and then, Royal Air Force.

Hmm.

On the one hand, images from fifth century BCE of Aphrodite carrying a dove. And the Acropolis decorated with relief figures of doves, and the temple of Aphrodite in Daphni. Don't the Roman goddesses Venus and Fortuna adorn themselves with doves? And in ancient Mesopotamia, doves are symbols of Inanna-Ishtar, the goddess of love, sexuality, and war.

And dove figurines in lead were discovered in the temple of Ishtar at Aššur, dating to the thirteenth century BCE, and a painted fresco from Syria shows a giant dove emerging from a palm tree in the temple of Ishtar, indicating that the goddess herself was sometimes believed to take the form of a dove.

I am getting a scholar's tour of ancient art history and religious studies now. The Talmud compares the spirit of God hovering over the waters to a dove that hovers over her young. In post-biblical Judaism, souls are envisioned as bird-like (Bahir 119), a concept that may be derived from the Biblical notion that dead spirits "chirp" (Isa. 29:4). The Guf, or Treasury of Souls, is sometimes described as a columbarium, a dove cote. A dove cote! This connects it to a related legend: the "Palace of the Bird's Nest", the dwelling place of the Messiah's soul until his advent (Zohar II: 8a–9a). The Vilna Gaon explicitly declares that a dove is a symbol of the human soul (Commentary to Jonah, 1). The dove is also a symbol of the people Israel (Song of Songs Rabbah 2:14), an image frequently repeated in Midrash.

Now here is the Bible. I summarize for us! The symbolism of the dove in Christianity is first found in the Old Testament Book of Genesis in the story of Noah's Ark, "And the dove came in to him at eventide; and, lo, in her mouth an olive-leaf plucked off: so Noah knew that the waters were abated from off the earth." Genesis 8:11 And, also, in the New Testament Gospels of Matthew and Luke, both passages describe after the baptism of Jesus, respectively, as follows, "And Jesus when he was baptized, went up straightway from the water: and lo, the heavens were opened unto him, and he saw the Spirit of God descending as a dove, and coming upon him." Matthew 3:16 and, "And the Holy Spirit descended on him in bodily form like a dove. And a voice came from heaven: "You are my Son, whom I love; with you I am well pleased." Luke 3:22 The Holy Spirit descending on Jesus and appearing in the bodily form of a dove is mentioned in the other two Gospels as well (see Mark 1:10 and John 1:32).

The use of a dove and olive branch as a symbol of peace originated with the early Christians, who portrayed the act of baptism accompanied by a dove holding an olive branch in its beak, and also used the image on their sepulchres.

I read about how Christians derived the symbol of the dove and olive branch from Greek thought, including its use of the symbol of the olive branch, and the story of Noah and the Flood. In Christian Iconography, a dove also symbolizes the Holy Spirit, in reference to Matthew 3:16 and Luke 3:22 where the Holy Spirit is compared to a dove at the Baptism of Jesus.

And then how the early Christians in Rome incorporated into their funerary art the image of a dove carrying an olive branch, often accompanied by the word "Peace". It seems that they derived this image from the simile in the Gospels, combining it with the symbol of the olive branch, which had been used to represent peace by the Greeks and Romans.

In the earliest Christian art, the dove represented the peace of the soul rather than civil peace, but from the third century it began to appear in depictions of conflict in the Old Testament, such as Noah and the Ark, and in the Apocrypha, such as Daniel and the lions, the three young men in the furnace, and Susannah and the Elders.

Before the Peace of Constantine (313 AD), in which Rome ceased its persecution of Christians following Constantine's conversion, Noah was normally shown in an attitude of prayer, a dove with an olive branch flying toward him or alighting on his outstretched hand. According to Graydon Snyder, "The Noah story afforded the early Christian community an opportunity to express piety and peace in a vessel that withstood the threatening environment" of Roman persecution. Medieval illuminated manuscripts, such as the Holkham Bible, showed the dove returning to Noah with a branch. Wycliffe's Bible, which translated the Vulgate into English in the 14th century, uses "a braunche of olyue tre with greene leeuys" ("a branch of olive tree with green leaves") in Gen. 8:11. In the Middle Ages, some Jewish illuminated manuscripts also showed Noah's dove with an olive branch, for example, the Golden Haggadah (about 1420).

Doves and the pigeon family in general are respected and favored because they are believed to have assisted the final prophet of Islam, Muhammad, in distracting his enemies outside the cave of Thaw'r, in the great Hijra. A pair of pigeons had built a nest and laid eggs at once, and a spider had woven cobwebs, which in the darkness of the night made the fugitives believe that Muhammad could not be in that cave.

And now I am thinking of the history of doves in all our history, on banners and in art, part of the Olympic Games, and Picasso's "La Colombe" drawing at an international peace conference. Picasso said that his father had taught him to paint doves to explain his philosophy: "I stand for life against death; I stand for peace against war."

Yet we come to military history. A caption:

> *"The rock dove is, due to its relation to the homing pigeon and thus communications, the main image in the crest of the Tactical Communications Wing, a body within the Royal Air Force."*

"Thus communications." I am trying to find out for us what it is about pigeons that makes them canny messengers. Apparently, their Mercury roles are electromagnetism, a "homing" ability to return to one's place. I read that it was discovered in fifth century Syria and Persia. Today scientists say pigeons can hear low frequencies, about 0.1 Hertz, using sound waves from earth as their guides, as acoustic maps.

Wait—Hertz. I have read about this—that love is so many Hertz. Let's see: "What does listening to 528 Hz do?"—posted on the internet. Answer: "According to Dr. Leonard Horowitz, 528 Hertz is a frequency that is central to the "musical mathematical matrix of creation." He calls it the "love frequency" and claims that it resonates at the heart of everything and "connects one's heart and spiritual essence to the spiraling reality of heaven and earth."

Then I read other questions people pose about pigeons: "Search for: <u>Do pigeons feel love?</u>

How do pigeons show affection?" Answer: "They are
very affectionate. Pigeons love to cuddle with each other and give their mate light pecks around the neck and head …. When one bird of a pair returns to a nest they often greet each other with very low, raspy coos." Then, "Is it safe to eat a pigeon?" "Can pigeons cry?" "Why do pigeons sit like humans?' "How do you bond with pigeons?" "How do you know if a pigeon is happy?"

I stare at an image of a pigeon, with patterns of waves and sea's brilliant green and sky's soft grey, imagining their sonar moxie. It is said that they not only delivered messages during our own times, remembered by my father in World War II, but they actually went to hospitals to deliver vials of fluids and blood.

So pigeons were crated, with baggage tags, shipped and then released on their destination, our knowing they would find their way back.

While I am processing this phenomenon, I scan questions posted on the internet, just as you are doing right now, such as "do carrier pigeons still exist?" (They did become extinct.) And here is one answer: "The English Carrier pigeon is a breed of domesticated pigeon that is descended from the rock dove. They are now bred as ornamental birds by pigeon fanciers."

There is much to learn, clearly I have so much to learn. Be with me here.

The pigeons are now kept, relegated to cages, bred for ornament, and squab, the baby pigeon, is listed on restaurant menus as a delicacy, and doves are not mentioned on the menu, but it is rock doves that are tasty, and hopefully they will not be eaten all at once.

When they are loved, as in *delicious*?

According to Sartre, each choice we make defines us while at the same time revealing to us what we think a human being should be.

Fellow pigeon fancier, as I suspect you are, as I trust you are, may this epistle home its way to you on wafts of encircling waves, let what you have to say to me return, as you are an earth whisperer, cooing to me of your love, and mine for you.

Let us let the shining-necked pigeons fly from their cages, and figure out the next step of how to once again make iridescent our skies with their messages from the gods of what we need to know for the next ten thousand years, a fleet extending olive branches on behalf of earth's creatures that can tell us all about what it is to be useful, as well as beautiful, on earth.

BUFFALO

Buffalo Poem

The buffalo returned last night.

Hooves pounded the tin roof.
I could hear myself trampled,
a valley trembling with thunder,
my ears filled with sounds,
and my mind spill awoke me,
flooded with rain in the night.

Is it because I am a woman I can be filled up,
like a bowl or a cup,
even awake?
As my dream receded
I was a lake,
and the rain poured into me.
I was nothing
but the sound of the stampede.

And it was night, and rain.

But in the morning, only birds.

Outside on the plain there is a straggly green,
broken toothpicks, left by the herd.

Although I look for buffalo in vain,
there are only plops, and puddles.

And this grass now,
which would not grow for me,
but is there for buffalo?

The buffalo return, bring Spring.

And I, hollowed out in brown season
like ripe scooped cantaloupe,
renounce all doubt:
I see no earthly reason
why I cannot hope
that being so filled
with spring sounds—
I too will pound.

BEAR (again)

A bear attacks a woman.
She fights it off — with her laptop

(CNN) – A Southern California teen had a rude awakening when an outdoor nap turned into a bear attack. She survived by fighting the bear off with her only weapon – a laptop. The 19-year old Sierra Madre woman fell asleep in backyard chair Monday evening, Fish and Wildlife Capt. Patrick Foy told CNN. "She awoke to the sound of a bear approaching her," Foy said. "It immediately attacked." The bear scratched the young woman's arms and legs, but then it began to bite her leg. Her wounds were not life-threatening. "The only weapon she had was her laptop. She hit the bear with it and stunned it long enough to escape inside the house," Foy said. "She fought back vigorously, which is what you should do with any wildlife in California." Local police responded to the incident, followed soon by wildlife officers. Bear tracks nearby and a glimpse of a bear around midnight provided evidence corroborating her story. "This was an unprovoked, aggressive attack," Foy said. The woman did not have any food, and did not get between a bear and her cubs. "It's likely she was looked at as prey," Foy speculated. The bear that attacked the woman has not yet been found.

There is a lot in this story that speaks to me, and I am sure to you, too, although you may not have grown up in this neighborhood and do not live currently in a situation in which you may be beset by bears, at least as far as you know. But that is the point. We fall asleep, drowsy and forgiving ourselves our idleness after reading James Wright's "Lying in a Hammock" poem trying not to waste our life. Or we are reading Mary Oliver, following her "Instructions for Living a Life" and down with her on the grass gazing at grasshoppers so that we do not waste our "one wild and precious life." We are Zen, as well as exhausted, and we know Wendell Berry, and Jane Hirschfield, and Linda Gregg, and Joy Harjo would approve, and Emily Dickinson, well, she would understand. We are writing, perhaps like John Muir, who was trying to transcribe the universe as it manifests (and succeeded, my mother would say). Emerson approves in every other sentence of his imprecations—the others he urges us to action); we are in the grove, the ancient grove, and it is Horace, it is lyric, it is Eden, it is the Garden. We are golden; it is Woodstock. Joni Mitchell strums. And then the next thing we know, fur is in our face.

We have conjured the wilderness itself, the wildness in all these words we read and write. And we are contending, we who only read about contending, Odysseus the great contender in all things, but now it is us, really, contending, and it is real.

We don't believe it, though. How can we believe it?

We're in our backyards, as safe as safe can be, in an idyll! And now we're wrestling with a creature who doesn't play by the rules, who bites below the waist, and the next thing we know—we're looking for weapons, the Starbucks mug will not do, we use the only thing we have, our laptop. We clunk it on the snout of the bear (am I really slamming down my word doc on a bear?), we are cringing with regret, we were raised to carry spiders outside, as we take that laptop and swing it once again, hard, against the ear and jaw of the bear, who is right now trying to bite our arm.

Why, why, we are asking, still in shock at being so woken, and now we're standing up, to get a better leverage to pound that bear's head.

There is a lot to unpack in this story, as we read (in the safety of our bedroom).

Sitting down and reading and writing makes one "prey." This we did not know. The life of our minds as we express ourselves and learn of each other's hearts and thoughts is the equivalent of "eat me—now." The bear escaped—it is still out there.

You, reading this, me, writing this, we are in this together. We can know the world is wild yet, inside and out, it is sprouting through all the cracks in civilization, and there is no place safe, nothing that is not dangerous, but how we live it.

WORM

You Have This Chance

On my watch
a worm—
now the mind stops,
as I stop
to not step on it—
moves
in mauveness,
against the grey wet sidewalk.

It—

again my mind stops,
pauses, pauses as well as stops,
searching for the word to describe
how this happening fellow mortal is there
and there and there
across space and time,
slithers, *inches*, we say, these verbs
for how a straw-like cylinder
moves forward
imperceptibly
as I track its progress
against the two brown seeds on the sidewalk
which shine with rainlight
in the morning light.

It
expands itself,
forwards and backwards,
as it moves
in one direction,
taking its immense self,
its huge self, its majestic self,
forward
in some way
I can't describe.

                              It
                       is so beautiful,
                        so mysterious,
              in how it expands and stretches,
                  and it is making progress,
           it is going across the sidewalk, where?
               Where are you going, my precious?
                   Do you know you are at risk?
                    Anyone could step on you!

                        O, what misfortune,
           to squash the life of such an extraordinary being!

                               I
         step around, saying, good luck to you, my friend,
                    and good luck to everyone,
            that we may not stop the purpose of this worm,
              this morning that has started out with awe!
                   With gratitude for this life—
                     to live with such phenomena.

                And then the brown sidewalk leaves,
                      whom we do step upon,
                            now torn,
                 and shining in the morning rain,
                      singing to me, we, too,
                        we are so beautiful.

And even though our movement is over,
that you can see,
we are still here,
with some purpose on earth, still.

We have a long way yet to go—
and who knows when it is over?

They are telling me so much.

Companions
in this our life,
worm, brown leaf,
their destinies are on my mind,
our dazzling journeys,
fates beyond the morning light.

FLAMINGO

My Not My Flamingo

Who owns the land?

Faulkner asked, *who owns the land*?
It was in a story called *The Bear* with a dog called Lion.

But hasn't this been the human question since creation,
isn't this question why people kill each other,
why all creatures for that matter kill each other:
territory?
The sandbox: *mine.*

But we have worried this question since we've been telling stories,
singing songs,
scratching on leaves and stones and bark a conscience.
Peter, Paul, and Mary, singing Woody Guthrie's,
This Land Is Your Land, This Land is My Land

Perhaps we don't own the land and Gilgamesh,
2700 BCE, had it right:
the gods do.
We cut down forests
and declare ownership
at our peril.

Emily Dickinson who did not get a Nobel Prize,
asked this before there was a Nobel Prize.
In her slant sly way,
saying, of course the King is a legal owner of the land,
But God be with the Clown.
The Clown doesn't think he owns it,
he only sees it and loves it *as if it were his own.*

But when I reread *Alice in Wonderland*
again after all these years,
a professor now ready to teach my class at Oxford University,
and came to the chapter which begins,

The chief difficulty Alice found at first was in managing her flamingo: she succeeded in getting its body tucked away, comfortably enough, under her arm, with its legs hanging down, but generally, just as she had got its neck nicely straightened out, and was going to give the hedgehog a blow with its head, it *would* twist itself round and look up in her face, with such a puzzled expression that she could not help bursting out laughing: and when she had got its head down, and was going to begin again, it was very provoking to find that the hedgehog had unrolled itself, and was in the act of crawling away: besides all this, there was generally a ridge or furrow in the way wherever she wanted to send the hedgehog to, and, as the doubled-up soldiers were always getting up and walking off to other parts of the ground, Alice soon came to the conclusion that it was a very difficult game indeed.

I am weeping.

Yes!
The flamingo thrust into your arms
to play this game of mortal life.
It is so clear to me, all at once,
this truth.

What is your Flamingo,
I asked my students as they joined me that morning
pondering in the tavern on the campus quad,
where we meet to discuss Revolutionary Imagination.

As they told us their Flamingo,
what they contend with in their lives.
everyone cried.

Our Flamingos, I said,
what is thrust into our arms,
what wriggles and flails.

Then I remembered,
Who owns the land?
The fate of Enkidu and Gilgamesh, and Adam and Eve,

Emily Dickinson's Clown,
all the stories we tell ourselves to say
nothing of earth is ours.

Perhaps this could be
what Emerson meant when he said
"the me and the not me."

There is the us who is not us,
that we have been given,
that we do not own,
and will return.
Then there is the us that always was,
the spirit us who sings,
the us with wings who belongs to this world,
this infinitely happening world,
this immeasurable beauty.

I can't tell the difference.

No! No! Whitman says,
"The brood of the turkey-hen and she with her half-spread wings,
I see in them and myself the same old law."

The "not me" is the beloved of this world,
whom I must adore,
this wriggling flamingo I do not own,
cannot hold,
yet hold dear,
and it goes with my plaid pink shoes.

EARTH

In Which It Is Revealed I Am Earth

I have no idea how to think about my body,
huddled and cold and cramped;
I just know it aches.

Some stricken landscape.

You touch me.

At first I'm plains, their buffalo, hump, hunched,
then land itself, as hands root out
stumps in my spine,
gnarled nests in my shoulders,
boulders and burls in my arms,
and I find myself feeling grateful I have a back,
that we are covered with flesh,
even our skull,
we are draped with flesh over rock,

My flesh is river, a wild Merced, flowing over rocks,
I am moving, a current—
and then my bones begin to sing,
my shoulder sags and droops
as I breathe deeply,
lavender and pine.

I am a ribbon, loose, untied,
a flag unfurled, a present that is opened.

My bones are music,
and my feet are on the line:
I pick up my cell phone, who is this?
It's my toes,
and my arches grab the phone.

Now everyone is talking, thighs, muscles, knees, ears,
a waking up like sunrise to the birds.

And then, suddenly,
Silence, and it is just I,
this slab of solace,
and hands never stopping,
instructing the pain,
my flesh is listening to these firm hands.

I keep my eyes closed,
imagining myself whatever this is—
not these bones and aches and flesh—
just the warmth, that is all I am,
just the warmth—
in a sea floating like kelp,
moving with the current.

How ancient is this practice, laying on of hands?

It is as old as wind in grass, and I am flowing.
Perhaps I am a field as the wind moves through me.

I keep my eyes shut,
and feel light, light.

I think, light is what a geranium knows,
and light is being,
when you no longer are heavy and hard as stone,
and no longer own the pain
and the stiff struggle against gravity.

Light is a dolphin carrying me,
no longer flesh and bone,
but buoyant spirit,
warm, warm rising in the morning sun.

As if it were his Own! –
Emily Dickinson

SUNSHINE

E=mc2—For Example, You Are My Sunshine

Who loves you?
If you're needed, that's a clue.
Think of how you matter.
To earth, for example.
Earth goes all out for you.
It dishes up sunrise,
it plates sunset,
for example, every day,
the original delivery service of chocolate and roses,
Valentine messages of Be Mine,
I'm Yours,
outlandish and lavish displays for your notice,
some peacock's tail spread—
yes, yes, it wants to mate with you, that is for sure.
Maybe not right now but some time,
some celestial dazzling union.
Or reunion.

Right now it wants an engagement with you.
If only you are impressed, and amazed.
It needs your knocked out notice.
It needs you dazed in a hammock,
caught off guard by rainbow,
rain's gleamy golden ginkgo on the pavement.

It is your beholding eyes
and lifted spirit that spring the rivers,
your sways to its strings and wind instruments
that pulse the tides,
your obsession with lemon pie that grows the grass,
your love of light on seas that makes it tilt and spin and spin and spin and spin.

That is how much your sweet heart,
your wondering eyes,
your grateful ears,
are needed.
And that's just earth.
One example only,
how you matter.

NEBULAE

Frolic King Among the Nebulae
To Nicolino, 1980-2020

It is hard to fathom, and seems almost wrong to even try to wrap your head around this kind of beauty. The scale of this beauty. These structures dwarf our whole galaxy ... the eclipse of our sun by our moon is a good indicator of the scale for perspective ... meaning, the size of us, our eyeball relative to the earth relative to the moon relative to our star relative to our galaxy... our eyeballs just don't seem to be designed for experiencing galactic beauty, our bodies in general are not good for frolicking in the æther, but our consciousness is perfect for that, and therefore I hope one day to frolic about all the nebulas. Love you. — Nico Moss, 2017.

A star's life is a constant struggle against the force of gravity.
– NASA Education Website

It's not possible to know
if you can actually frolic
without gravity.

Is it?

When you imagine frolicking
don't you see leaping about,
defiance against gravity's laws?

So you need to be earth bound,
imprisoned,
to break free here and there,
now and then.

You need props for unlawful behavior.
Ribbons and baskets and hats
and striped shoes and music—
a flute and fiddle.

Meanwhile you tell me it's all energy,
a vibrational universe.

So I don't know what being in the nebulae is like,
  this place of star birth,
 or what happens to gravity,
  when sound is light.

Gravity is needed for stars to become,
 and there has to be enough
  to warrant serious frolicking.

We say in sad times the situation is *grave*.

 What is going to spring matter?
  It has to be grave enough.
  It has to have gravitas.

Frolicking only makes sense in this case,
  after a death,
when it is understood that it is called for
to kick up one's heels and swirl and whirl
  into so much shining dust,
   to spin and spin,
   becoming a star,
  as you are, as you are.

As you knew you would.

RIVER (again)

Don't Even Read This

The river says
Don't look at your phone!
Look at me!
Listen!

The sky says here is Top of the Hour news.
The rocks shining with water in the afternoon light
So bright it is black and white
Say this is What's Trending.

Under Fashion
it's this season's leaves coming out
The trees turning green in newest shades.

Tech Report
is the train whistle as I sit on the bridge
and hear the water sigh and swish
and shhhhhh and hiss
and it's an engine
of the universe
fueled by light.

And wind.
breaking news the breeze.

Read More
and I read more,
I breathe in.

This story catches my eye—
water flowing over rock
a miniature Niagara Falls
and in the flow
a quiet pool over which a heron stands peering in.
Two geese flying low.

I have forgotten what I have to worry about or dread.
I can't remember what someone said
that made me sad
for me and my family and our species.

Such news—
Earth says read me.
Look up!
Oh, Fellow Mortal, look around!

See me! See us! Oh, listen!
And I who was removed from the sixth-grade choir
because I could not sing,
although I love to sing,
I was singing.
We all were singing.

It is great news.
I realize I am happy.
.
For now
inside this moment
alive.

JACARANDA

I Am Telling You This

I'm Nobody Emily Dickinson said and it was more
than what the sly Odysseus said to escape the Cyclops.

I know what she meant, now,
because I cannot find my underwear—
and what he meant too,
getting the better of the Cyclops—any underwear,
I cannot find any of my underwear,
I am writing this Commando.

I don't know why I am telling you this.
I don't know if you have ever read a poem
whose lines were authored Commando.
(Are you saying, ahhhg, can you tell?)
One day this past week, in fact, Graduation Day,
this is what I could not find.
My graduation robe.
My Ph.D. hood that goes with it.
My underwear. My earrings.

Today, I have lost my journal.
I don't know where I left it.
I drove 45 miles across town,
and it took two hours,
this is Los Angeles,
west side to east side,
and over the mountains in the middle,
to go back to the store where I thought I left it.
This is the nakedest feeling of all,
even more than my ears without my earrings.

I think it has to do with the magnetic belts,
and these are things that are re-absorbed
by the energy fields along with socks and pens.

But I wonder if it is seemly for a sixty-four-year old woman
to be losing her underpants
and going around without any
and telling you this.

How not lost but hopeful it is
when everything
is leaving you as Mars' seas took off,
how you become Nobody
and how marvelous that everything is possible
and no one knows how you are living
the epic power
of Commando.

This means that gravity is no longer a force in your life.

Scurrilous driving home on the streets
lined with Jacaranda in full purple bloom,
astonishing against the blue sky,
purples the grey paved street,
and I think of Alice Walker,
what she said about the color purple,
and I think of God,
and how on the TED talk
describing genius
as the Muse from without,
from the gods—
the gods!—asking you to write a poem,
we are told to believe in the world asking this of you,
and is this something in the realm of the sacred
that I should write.

Certainly it is what I am thinking about,
driving home in my white Impala
my dad got in memory of my red Chevy '58,
the two guys in the red race car next to me,
looking me over,

how is it that this same mind whoofed by the sacred call of Muse
is Commando in this world
and no one knows,
no one knows
how we are called,
or in what state,
no one ever knows when you are Commando.

But it changes everything, right here, right now.

BASKET

Natural History Does Not
Include My Plans to Fly

I don't know what I expected,
in this Museum of Natural History
which turns out to be death.

Pterodactyl,
bound in concrete,
a city block of bone beams—tethered and classified.
Shutter wings.

Inside, the walls are soiled above the hand-rails,
bannisters oiled by grasping palms,
stairways smell of sweating feet.
Two giggling boys cuff each other on the landing.

Once it flew.

Now grounded with mementos,
stuffed buffalo,
animal antiques,
mangy remnants of the ice age.

From continent to continent,
in canoes,
on sailboats,
on rafts,
we trudge through our history.

Five hundred years in a room
and we ascend the stairs,
winding and winding,
room after room,
always to meet the same eyes of the hunter,
skins of the hunted,
remains.

Clutter brings me down—baskets,
thousands of years of them,
brown triangles,
some poor lady's time—
oh her time!
in stifling caves,
on the cliffs,
on the ice,
confining plains.

Fringed leather.
Dead rabbits.

There are artifacts
but these are not facts.

No, no. None of this is real.
I deny a history of skeletons.
I don't have bones.
No spine, no relic,
to say if you live,
you die.

I own a private evolution.

This is my time now,
my baskets,
my mysterious flesh.

PETAL

the song sings itself—Wm. Carlos Williams

When the sun floods in it feels like wealth
in the richest dwelling in the world.

Who can deny my house is grandeur itself in such light?

When the camellia blossom falls off in early spring winds
in twirls and swirls,
it has watched the birds so long
it thinks it is finally flying.

Who wants to tell it that it isn't?

Who knows what is flying anyway?
Or singing which may be the same thing?
The way the spirit can be lifted from the body,
And all gravity's laws—

Perhaps it truly is flying
Singing or falling blossom.

Perhaps birds are petals,
From some flowering tree,
Free at last.

HUMMINGBIRD

On Being Human

Journal. It strikes me, nov, 22 2023, 7:18 am, not dark, not quite light, going outside in bare feet to take out cheese that got moldy to still make it for the trash pickup, looking at the garden as I'm going in, the olive tree, with some astonishment and wonder, it is finally beginning to look like a tree.

It has olives, it is branching out, it is fuller, it is getting taller,
it is becoming an olive tree, from some little bush we planted, and it knows how to do this, that is what I was thinking with wonder, it knows how to do this complicated business of becoming thicker, the branches, wider and longer, and to make leaves, and have leaves grow bigger, and olives, actual olives, and taller, and I look at the fig tree, now shorn of leaves, one dark brown leaf droopy, hanging on, and it knows how to shed its leaves, and when,
and these miraculous beings, they all know what to do.

Not one of them has a dream like I did last night of being on a stage, with all these friendly people awaiting my performing nursery rhymes, all excited, every seat taken, as I realized I did not know what I was going to talk about, that at some point I had had some idea, but now did not know at all what I had in mind.

And is that our lives, our days, as we revolve again about the sun, and don't know our lines, our moves, and I am sure the squirrels and chestnut tree and jay do not say, what should I do, what will become of me? Which is what you and I do, every day.

That is being human, a great brain that has this fantastic opportunity to do justice to this . . . gift of consciousness, of being on earth, a fellow mortal or fellow entity (I think of rocks, and their evolution of being, their path of continuous becoming).

We question ourselves, we experience unknowing, bewilderment, bafflement, worry, we don't know, even as our bodies, they are nature, they mysteriously grow, do all the things we have no idea of, at least not me, my cells and veins and arteries and all that happens, I can't even place what it is inside that makes me itch in my sternum, below my breasts, or contort and cramp, what is that, I don't know the difference between my spleen and liver and kidney and how it all works, the miles of tubes, and still my heart beating as I write this, my eyes focusing, they know what to do, my fingernails grow, my wounds heal, my skin wrinkles, in some mysterious process, and yet my mind, my mind wonders at the coming day, becoming day, how do I do this, what do I say, how to make something of this day, worthy of existence? And my students who are so bright, they ask this, and I at 75 ask this, still yearning to become, not knowing my lines, even though I've been given a stage.

Even here, I am given a page, and I ponder what to say that is what needs to be said.

At this stage of our lives.

"All the world's a stage . . . "—Shakespeare, and we are "merely actors in it," but that means we have lines, a director, and the truth is, we don't know our lines.

I was once directing a play in the summer program of the Y in downtown Pasadena near City Hall, a Dramathon for girls ages 5-14, and it was the day of the performances, and a little girl was crying.

I bent down, and said, my arms reaching out, why are you crying? I don't know my lines, she said. What part are you, I asked. I'm a bush.

Well there it is—because the bush may not know its lines, but it does know what to do! Whereas in the way we are as humans, we don't know our lines, and unlike the bush, who, as far as we know, does not have a voice, we have speaking parts in this our life.

But what are these lines? We strive to know. We read and listen to the poets, our Virgil, who write their lines with passion and authority, and we recite these to ourselves, and they get us through the moments. But otherwise we are on our own.

I imagine the illustration of this journal entry as a willow tree on Chat with a balloon thought-shape over its head, asking "What are my lines?" "What to say?"

or even, "What to do today?" That's funny, right? Much less, or much more, to show worry, or fear. Oh, remorse, and guilt. Sorrow for what it has done, for what it has not done, for each other, and our earth.

That kind of sorrow, anguish, regret, pain, that hollowness within, so that inside we ring like a bell, which "tolls for thee," yes it does, Poet John Donne. That is human, not tree.

On this stage, on this page, I strive to honor the Muse, to know my lines, what to utter, as knowing as the olive tree, the willow, the pine, who know what to do when, to be so stately, to move magnificently in the wind, each tree its own way of flutter, to know how to grow up and down at the same time, to extend in angles and curves, out, and out, to bring forth what is inside, to sprout the leaf, the fruit, with its seeds of new life, rebirth, and when to turn yellow and gold and crimson and vermilion, or not, remain green, and when to fly, when to let gravity take us back to earth, when to let go of one's leaves, and stand there bare, in the rain and cold and snow, to bear again the sap running and the leaves unfurled. To put amazing into word, we, who live with miracle and mystery, is this why *God be with the Clown*, why we ponder? Like the hummingbird who brings news of my lost ones, alive again, and me, alive again, in its curious stare.

TURTLE, et.al.

Alive Again Today

i who have died am alive again today.
E.E. CUMMINGS

*Dear March — Come in —
How glad I am —
I hoped for you before —
Put down your Hat —
You must have walked —
How out of Breath you are —
Dear March, how are you, and the Rest —
Did you leave Nature well —
Oh March, Come right upstairs with me —
I have so much to tell.*
EMILY DICKINSON

Dear March,
you picked up your hat,
you are leaving —

there is more to tell you —
that April — lock the Door!

O March! Lucky the turtle
who was rescued from the highway
by my mother, father, and sister
making their way across the country
to encounter our wild relatives,
each stranger than the last,
and picking up and naming Lucky
was the only thing they agreed upon.

They became stranger to each other on that long road trip,
and were not speaking to each other.

My sister in the back seat
conveyed their messages back and forth.

But when they found Lucky
no words were needed—
that Fellow Mortal story—
and doing the Bunny Hop with Sophia
on the train platform in Burlington, Vermont,
at 5:30 am as the snow fell,
she would dance with me anywhere
at the drop of a hat,
including the Trader Joe's
we got kicked out of for dancing in the aisles,
(well, they were playing bouncy music),

and the story of Apples and Moley our English Setters
and how we bought Apples
from the pastor who married us in the Indiana woods
while a truck circled with guns
(it was under a dogwood tree in bloom
and it was the 70's
and we didn't know we were trespassing
as we recited e.e. cummings'
"i thank You God for most this amazing" with its line,
"i who have died am alive again today)

and O March how Apples was hit by a car on Highway 37
outside White Cow Pasture,
our ramshackle house with the tin roof
on which rain pounded
like buffalo,
and so we bought her sister from Bobby Knight
the basketball coach,
and named her Moley,
and people said what is Moley short for and I said,
it's not short for anything,
it's long for Mole,
and that was because of *Wind in the Willows*

which I gave to Christer when we met
and decided to exchange books and declare ourselves
and as it turned out,
it was not such an odd choice
to give the man you knew you would marry,
however untamed,
because he gave me *Pan* by Knut Hamsun,
and Pan was in *Wind in the Willows*,
and we knew we on the same page,
and then Moley . . . O March—
who was alive like no one has ever been alive,
dying in my arms,
who taught me what it is to know a Fellow Mortal—

But March, forgive me—
Nicolino's orchid after four years suddenly blossomed,
I have to tell you that—
it is a miracle, heavens speaking to me,
yes, his spirit is here,
after years of waiting I finally told the orchid,
you don't have to bloom,
you are perfect as you are,
And then it began to blossom—

and Sugarplum, my Siamese,
the subject of my first poem, My Cat Sugarplum,
at fourth grade on the Principal's wall.

And Daddy bringing me apples in his shirt
covered with ants, and Guthrie thinking they are divine,
and my thinking they are God,
and Lorry and me mowing the lawn
and what the ducks and chickens did to the daisies for the wedding
and Patty Ryan as our ducks and chickens on the loose
in her driveway
and how the racoon Eloise killed Beep Beep
and Daddy missed school because of death in the family
and his Principal asked when he returned who had died

and he said our duck and he was crying
and afterwards fired and evaluated for mental decline—
O March, O March—we were all crying,
she had just laid her eggs—I imprinted her at UCLA—
I have to tell you—

Oh, my jacket?
Yes, its bulging pockets—
once I left it at my parents.
They found it, and everyone was asking, whose is it,
and my mother said, look in the pockets,
if there are shells and pennies
and leaves and seed pods
it's Barbara's.

It was.

Here is your hat—
everything is alive again —
right here—your being here —
Dear March,
you came—you came!

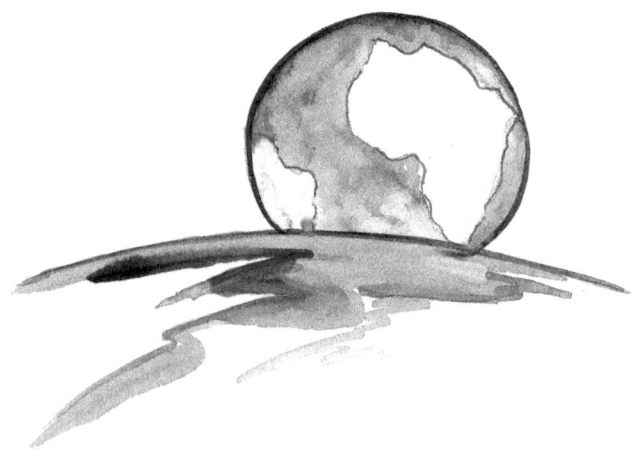

A Note from the Illustrator

CHRISTINE CROZIER — I am honored to be asked to illustrate **Clown Cantos**. Barbara's work radiates pure light and joy, lifting the spirit with every word. Her creativity invited me to soar alongside her, stretching my artistic wings beyond the familiar and into new realms of expression. I am grateful for this beautiful opportunity to explore and play with whimsy and delight. Thank you.

contactme@christinecrozier.com
www.christinecrozier.com

A Note from My Mother

You would think a mother should not have a voice in her daughter's work, especially in my case, since I am not "here." Because every mother would say, buy my daughter's book, it's the best! And it's not like I always approve of her bossy happiness, her insistent stance, wholly unaffected by dismay. Sometimes I lost my temper: once in exasperation I told the woman on the phone to whom I was reporting her lost swimsuit, "my daughter is a scatterbrain." Between us, raising her was a little trying. Because everything excites her!

But if everything is alive, then I am, too. And I would just like to say, since she is giving me this space, that I have known joy. I would always say, Nature is my joy. My joy in holding our chickens, their trembling warmth, feeling their warm eggs, lying on a warm rock, in Yosemite's Happy Isles, yes, that joy. The morning sky in Joshua Tree. The lone tree in the cemetery on Wall Street where I worked. In my own way, yes, I have been alive, and glad.

A Note from My Son

I told her, I would always be alive, just in a different way. I'm with her when she sees the hummingbird (yes, it's I), the anchor (our special icon), the elephant (she cries), the crystal (she's learning), when she hears music, when she sees images of the nebulae. Yes, I am frolicking there.

Acknowledgements

Our illustrator is renowned Christine Crozier, whose award-winning work is featured in the traveling and permanent collection of the Yosemite Museum, and seen in museums, art centers, galleries, exhibitions, and private collections, including art built into homes. She curates the peer-reviewed gallery at the Pacific Grove Public Library. I have been amazed at her mysterious work which captures our world's splendor, but even mindful of her nobler instincts, her commitment to this world's natural beauty, I might not have dared to ask her to illustrate this book were it not for her dedication to fruitcake, and lemon meringue pie. Such kindness towards fellow mortals, such generous creativity and careful love of what this world has to offer the whole hungry swooning human—gave me hope to ask. The illustrations for this book will be exhibited in art shows including at the Carmel Art Association.

The title *Everything Is Alive in Its Own Way* is inspired by Ian Chillag's program on Radiotopia, "Everything Is Alive," first brought to me by our son Nicolino, and Dolly Parton's song, "Everything Is Beautiful In Its Own Way," written by Dolly Parton, lyrics c Sony/ATV Music Publishing LLC.

"To a Mouse," Robert Burns, *Poems, Chiefly in the Scottish Dialect*, the Kilmarnock Edition, by John Wilson of Kilmarnock, 31 July 1786.

Emily Dickinson, *The Poems of Emily Dickinson: Reading Edition*, ed. R.W. Franklin (Harvard, 1998)

Poems span fifty years of publishing.

Some poems have developed in the Tupelo Press 30-30 Project (a digital media format for a poem a day for thirty days), including the poems of Camel and Roo.

Some poems build from *Here for the Present: A Grammar of Happiness in the Present Imperfect, Live from the Poet's Perch*, Pacific Grove Books, 2021.

"Fat Lady Flying," was published in an earlier version of "The Practical Humanities, Lessons from Professor Sphinx, and Yes, It is Rocket Science," *The Soul Does Not Specialize: The Case for Revaluing the Humanities and the Polyvalent Imagination*, eds. Stephen Aizenstat, Jennifer Leigh Selig, Dennis Patrick Slattery, Mandorla Press, 2012.

"To All We Secretly Love" has a first iteration in the Tupelo Press 30-30 Project and was published as "Avatar of Day" in *New Millennium Writings,* ed. Alexis Williams Carr, 2016.

"In Which I Happily Give Up," published as "In Which I Happily Give Up the Role of Fate" in *Sometimes the Woman in the Mirror Is Not You and other hopeful news postings*, Finishing Line Press, 2015

"Washing the Lake," first published for Midsummer in *Aamulehti, ed. Perti Pessonen* (Tampere, Finland), 21 June 1991.

"Natural History Does Not Include My Plans to Fly" published in an earlier form as "Bones and Flesh: Peabody Museum of Natural History," *Calapooya 8*, 1980.

"Why" published as "Love Poem for Christer," in *Myrrh, Mothwing, Smoke: Erotic Poems*, eds. Marie Gauthier and Jeffrey Levine, Tupelo Press, 2013.

"How I Am Taught Green," original version in *Passion for Place*, ed. Paola Berthoin, RisingLeaf Impressions, 2012.

"Quantum Happiness at Charlie's Boathouse," *If You Promise to Let Me Write This Down I'll Buy You an Ice Cream,* Buddy Press, 1992.

"Resurrection Shenanigans," published in an earlier version as "Resurrection: on the sighting by scientists of fox thought extinct, caught by remote camera leaping orangely," *Sometimes the Woman in the Mirror Is Not You and other hopeful news postings*, Finishing Line Press, 2015 and *Here for the Present: A Grammar of Happiness in the Present Imperfectt, Live from the Poet's Perch,* Park Place Publications, 2021.

"John Muir Takes a Sauna with the Finnish Ladies of Kuopio," published in earlier versions as "Book Me, Sir: John Muir Takes a Sauna with The Finnish Ladies of Kuopio," Olivet College, Grand Prize winner, Abbie M. Copps Award, 1994, and "John Muir Takes a Sauna with the Naked Ladies of Kuopio," *Here for the Present*, Park Place Publications, 2021.

"When I Die You Don't Have to Divert the River for Me" original version published in *Frontier Poetry*, 2020.

The 2019 Frontier Award for New Poets, judged by Ocean Vuong, Kovah Albar, and Eve L. Ewing.

"I Forgive Gravity," New Millennium Writings+Musepaper 2023.

It Takes a Village.

I am grateful to the historic civic culture of Pacific Grove, California, and the larger Peninsula of Carmel and Monterey, a generative everyday commitment to poetry and art built into the fabric of citizen life. Even the Mayor and City Council of the City of Pacific Grove, and the City Staff, and Board, Staff, and Friends of the Pacific Grove Public Library, have played major roles, making possible the logistics of the original position of Poet in Residence in the midst of all the gritty and complicated business of managing a city in the limelight and all its institutions.

Whitney Latham Lechich, a long-time P.G. writer, bequeathed her 1892 cottage to the city for poetry-related uses. I am indebted beyond measure for citizens who have taken up the cause of poetry in the civic space, grounded in the Pacific Grove Poetry Collective—the original mavens of civic poetry, Marge Jameson and the *Cedar Street Times*, Cathy Gable, Susie Joyce, Karin Locke—gifts, genius loci, treasures to community. Their visions of what a poet in residence is and can mean have generated and sustained poetry as a living presence, and are responsible for encouraging city voices cheering me on: each in specific ways and together have been generous with time and resources to build a program around poetry that serves the community. The Poetry Collective's shenanigans on behalf of poetry include but are not limited to designing and carrying off events at the Little House at Jewell Park, the Gazebo at Jewell Park, City Chambers, *Cedar Street Times*, Motorcycle Museum, Pacific Grove High School, First Fridays, art galleries (including Flash Mobs at Artisana and Pacific Grove Art Center), Pacific Grove Public Library, forming a chapter of the Emily Dickinson International Society and related events involving artists, musicians, visiting and local poets, generating a Rumi Society, Burns' dinners ... Diana Godwin as Director of the Library helped instrumentally in the evolution of the Poets Program, Charlene Williams took the mantle, and since then many in the community have stepped forward as I continue to serve in all the ways I can in my fifteenth year. The leadership of Patricia Hamilton brings it all together as she aligns her commitment to the city and dedication to our natural world in her publishing projects.

Many Fellow Mortals and institutions have inspired and supported this ongoing experiment of Green in civic life. Scott Sanders has been with me from the beginning and shown what it means to face life bravely and lovingly, to honor the world with a scientist's knowledge and a ministry serving spirit with words. Sandra Gilbert, Wendy Barker, and the poets I first read with, Louise Gluck, Diane Middlebrook, William Stafford, Sharon Olds, Dorianne Laux, and over the years leading to Walter Gropius and the folks at Canterbury Woods, Richard Flanagan, Steven Silveira, Mary Turk, and the Pacific Grove Public Library denizens with Charlene Williams and Angela Canales, the loyal friendship of all artistic endeavors of Teresa Basham, Karen Sharp, and the Carmel Women's Club, Robert Reese and the Cherry Center for the Arts, Michelle Crompton and the Osher Institute for Lifelong Learning—all the OLLIS, Jeannie Adams, Dr. Bonn202ie Gisel, Curator, Yosemite Conservation Heritage Center (former LeConte Memorial Lodge), Yosemite National Park, Larry Roberts at the Lilly Arctic, Milt Cox and Gregg Wentzell at the Lilly Conference on College and University Teaching, Professors Pam Baker and Dr. Dorothy Lloyd, California State University Monterey Bay, Charles Goodrich, Springcreek Project, Oregon State University, Markku Henriksson and Mikko Saikku, University of Helsinki, William Copeland and Terhi Molsa, Fulbright Commission, Finland, Dr. Yolanda Robinson, U.S. Foreign Service, Hal Ginsberg and Sara Hughes, KRXA 540AM/Radio Monterey, Zappa Johns, podcast Barbaramossberg.com, the *Monterey Herald*, the *Monterey Weekly*, *Carmel Pine Cone*, California Central Writers, Larry Haagqvist and Poetry Out Loud, Robert Marcum of The Works, the Original Bookies (Barbara and David Ehrenpreis, Janet Meier, Bonnie Clark), UCLA Department of Biochemistry and poetry supporter Dr. Cathy Clarke, the Emily Dickinson International Society, the International Leadership Association (and Fetzer Institute), the Fulbright Alumni Association, John Muir High School Alumni Association, Goddard College, Thoreau Society and Thoreau Farmhouse, Tupelo Press, Sally Hoover, and my Muir community, and my academic home, with my students, colleagues, staff, the University of Oregon: vibrant ethos for thinking of planetary life and Other. My students, friends, and colleagues in one vibrational blur spend their lives looking up and down and out and within, being amazed, being amazing.

Ah, my family, Fellow Mortals—on earth and heaven—singers and sung Christer, Nicolino, Sophia, with our crew for these carryings on, their poetry and sense of what is at stake in its being written, Steven and Cathy Clarke, Will Clashe and Connie Ann Clarke, Lorraine and Steve Young, Stephanie Rose Young and Neil Bailpayee, Brian Young, and Madeleine Faith Young and TJ Price.

Glinda Anderson, a good witch, who dwelled on Lighthouse Avenue, lit my way, setting me on this path of residency, and Christine Crozier—our famous illustrator and avatar of The Fruitcakes, with Cathy Gable. Lisa Crawford Watson, author, journalist, teacher, heralding these books. My Acorns! And Memoir Groups in Pacific Grove, CA, through the Public Library, Pasadena CA, through John Muir High School Alumni, and Concord, MA, through Thoreau Farmhouse The Write Connection. And in Eugene, my FPs, Book Group, The Roundtable, Fortnightly Club, Longview Street ones, the Clark Honors College denizens—students, faculty, staff, leadership team, our friends of fifty years, and Tsunami Books poets, Kim Stafford, all creating this ethos in which I dwell.

My gratitude to the 2024 team of Pacific Grove Public Library and its Foundation and Friends. And *it must be sung*: Patricia Hamilton, wise teacher on Fellow Mortals, author, and publisher, who is committed to making the voices of community heard in the midst of fires, pandemic, civic turmoil and Sargasso Seas, the civic spirit for whom Poetry is Front Line, an essential worker. She talks the walk in her publishing commitments for community. Maybe she hears the universe singing, as a plant whisperer, who sees the green in everything.

And to the Fellow Mortals who teach us as we peer into their magic mirror and see ourselves, beautiful in our own way, singing, maybe they are our Virgils, saving us in *this our life*.

Fat Lady Flying
To Ann R. Clarke 1920-2010

"Obviously a fat lady flying works against all natural proven laws (One, Two, and Three) of gravity."—Sir Isaac Newton, *Principae Naturalis Philosophica Mathematica*

(too full of despair) No, no, you say, it's not possible,
I can't.

Of course there are things that don't need to fly,
but you're not one of them.

With your sentence of death you share with frogs
and the heron in the marsh and the stars,
and you see them soar and float,
radiate and sing out in darkness,
consider: they soar and float,
radiate and sing out in darkness.

You have seen elephant swim,
hippo glide over river bottom,
orangutan swing through trees.
So you know the largeness of grace.

Don't look around, it's you I mean.
Not by hoist, not heft, or heave, cranked by harness,
this is not physics of motion.

I'm not sure but my guess is to breathe.

There's a way of holding breath,
and it has to do with your eyes in this line,
imagining the fat lady flying who doesn't even try,
when she laughs and takes in the world,
its splinters and pebbles, its cries and sagging truths,
it's such a relief the world exhales
and she just rises.

That's you,
how I see you,
flying,
in these lines,
wind flows through you,
and what you hear now is your own voice,
its awed silence,
singing and rising over the world.

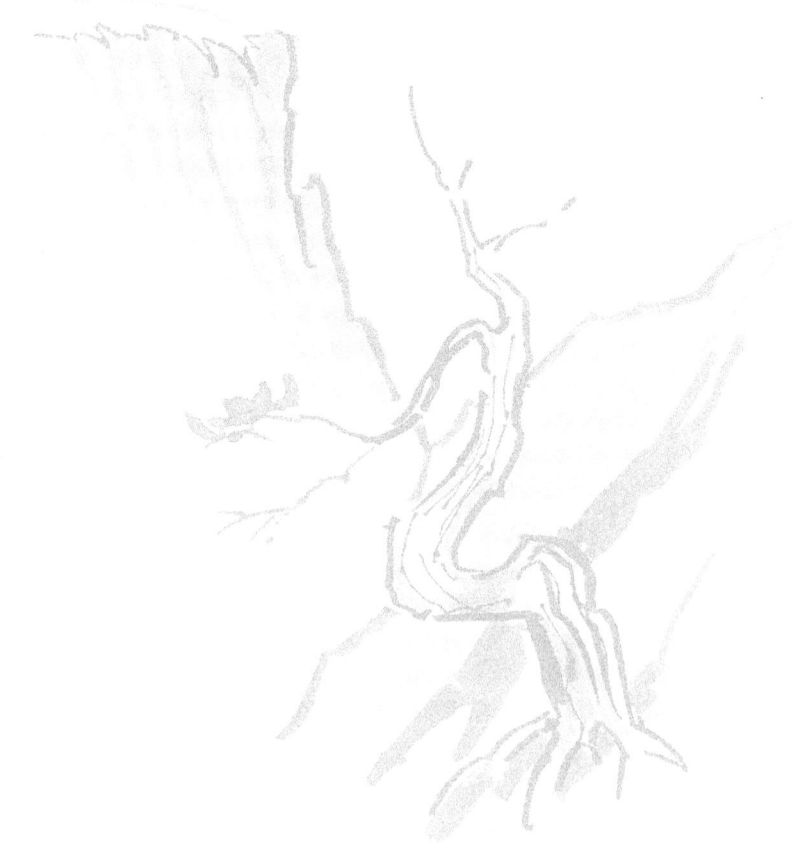

About the Author

BARBARA MOSSBERG is dedicated to poetry in the civic ethos ("no place safe from poetry"), which she defines as literary imagination applied to all things Life, in entrepreneurial roles ranging from college president, poet laureate, university professor, international lecturer, humanities activist, cultural diplomat, dramaturg, playwright, actor, literary critic, scholar, and radio host. And mother, buddy, friend, partner in this our journey.

Originally a driveway neighborhood puppeteer, she teaches, writes, and lectures on creativity in cultural and scientific leadership, environmental history, women's studies, and inspiration, for scholarly studies, academic and professional conferences, memoir workshops, leadership retreats, and public events. She is featured as a Senior Distinguished Fulbright Lecturer and Fulbright Specialist, holder of the Bicentennial Chair of American Studies at the University of Helsinki, cultural diplomat as U.S. Scholar in Residence in the federal appointment for USIA (American Studies Specialist), poet and writer in residence for multiple organizations, leader for fundraisers, launches, and civic occasions, and in productions of drama and musicals on cultural figures (including her original pieces for the Willows Theater and Cherry Center for the Arts on John Muir, Yosemite National Park summer speakers program, "Trees!" workshopped for the John Muir High School Springfest, "The Glory! Loving John Muir" for the Pasadena Heritage Society, "Emily Dickinson's Pop Up Kitchen" at numerous venues), and her own autobiographical "Fat Lady Flying" and "If You Promise To Let Me Write This Down I'll Buy You Ice Cream" for the

Jambalaya Playwrighting Festival at the Cherry Center (Carmel, CA). President of the Outdoors Theater Guild in Carmel, California, and founding Dean of the College of Arts, Humanities, and Social Sciences at California State University Monterey Bay, she provided leadership for community theater for over ten years.

Mossberg develops and leads memoir writing workshops for The Thoreau Farmhouse Trust (including its Wild Acorns), Pacific Grove Public Library, and others. These workshops use literature as prompts to invoke transformational writing for people's own voices at threshold moments as they write their own lives.

As a dramaturg for companies specializing in women's poets (The New Umbrella) and cultural genius (Ballet Fantastique), she engages audiences and companies including Off-Broadway's 59E59, Carmel Cherry Center for the Arts, Oxford (UK) Playhouse, and the Eugene Hult Center.

Dr. Mossberg (B.A. UCLA, M.A. and Ph.D. Indiana University) is President Emerita of Goddard College, California Laureate, City Poet Emerita, Pacific Grove (CA), Professor of Practice at Clark Honors College, University of Oregon, where she teaches creativity fusing literature and science, in "Eco literature and the Green Imagination," Revolutionary Imagination, Emerson and Einstein, Thinking Like the Sun, The Art of Living, Epic Influences: Poetry, Leadership, and You, The Power of Story, John Muir's Backpack, What Drama!, and new courses to inspire a sense of responsibility and hope for each other and our earth.

Since 2008 she has been creator and host of the weekly hour **Poetry Slow Down** (Talk Radio KRXA 540 AM, radiomonterey.com, podcast BarbaraMossberg.com). Seen on YouTube in poetry slams ("old lady moxie, strutting her poetic gear"), poetry flash mobs, Occupy movements, lit and pub crawls, blogs on Art&Culture for *Huffington Post*. Mossberg does "performative scholarship" on the writer's transformational cultural leadership; she celebrates the power of the word to change the world. She lectures worldwide in over twenty countries on poetry and culture ranging from Yosemite National Park and Oregon Country Fair to over 200 universities including Chulalongkorn (Bangkok), Mohammed V (Rabat), Charles (Prague), Oxford, Helsinki, Stockholm. She teaches study abroad in London, Oxford, Dublin, and Paris.

Mossberg is a founder of the Emily Dickinson International Society, serving as President of the Board and Director of Fundraising.

A prizewinning poet, teacher, and scholar, Mossberg's book on *Emily Dickinson When a Writer Is A Daughter* (Indiana, 1982) was *Choice* Outstanding Book of the Year in 1982. Her book *Clown Cantos: Everything Is Alive In Its Own Way / Meditations with Fellow Mortals* (Pacific Grove Books) is a sequel to *Here for the Present: A Grammar of Happiness in the Present Imperfect, Live from the Poet's Perch* (Pacific Grove Books). Mossberg is a contributor to Tupelo Press erotic poems anthology, *Myrrh, Mothwing, Smoke*, Tupelo's February 2014 and September 2015 on-line 30-30 Project, and Spring Creek Trillium Project / Writer in Residence at Shotpouch Creek, and Writer in Residence at Thoreau's Birth Room for the Thoreau Farmhouse Trust; recent work is in *Frontier Poetry* (Award for New Poets Series), Finishing Line Press New Women's Voices Series, *Sometimes the Woman in the Mirror Is Not You* (2015), and in *New Millennium Writings, Cider Press Review, Tupelo Quarterly Launch Edition, Cedar Street Times,* and others; she has recognition from New Millennium Writing, the Arts & Letters Rumi Prize, Snowbound Chapbook Award, Sunken Gardens Chapbook Award, and Word Works Washington Prize, and is Abbie M. Copps Grandprize Winner (twice) for Olivet College. She has been part of Colrain's and Tupelo's Manuscript Conferences, an invited speaker for poetry retreats with Aspen Institute, Fetzer Institute, A Room of Her Own (Ghost Ranch, NM), In Claritas (Assisi and Bari, Italy), Lilly Arctic Institute, Dublin Abroad Writers Conference, for the International Leadership Association (London, Prague, Denver, Asilomar), and as a poet at fundraisers for environmental, educational, and civic causes. Starting professionally at age twelve ($2 for a poem in a newspaper on the revolutionary war in Massachusetts), Mossberg has published poetry and criticism continuously for over fifty years. Her research on creativity and aging, Three Feet in the Afternoon, focuses on literary imagination from ages 50 to 105.

As a writer of ecological literacy, Mossberg models herself on Emily Dickinson's Clown, a responsible role to inspire hope in all ages. In such vein, she equally performs and engages in small-scale events and formal lecture venues or theaters, for eighteen people or eighteen hundred, each to her a "tremendous scene."

Barbaramossberg.com
Barbara.mossberg@gmail.com
honors.uoregon.edu/corefaculty

www.ingramcontent.com/pod-product-compliance
Lightning Source LLC
Chambersburg PA
CBHW061758070526
44586CB00023B/2616